the
devotional
poems of
FLORENCE FERN
AUSTIN-WALLACE

EDITED BY
GARY WALLACE

OWL ROOM
press

Copyright ©2019 Owl Room Press
ISBN: 978-0-578-61915-6
Cover & interior by Rocketship Graphic Design
Poem transcription by Vicki Ropp, Dennis Ropp, and Tai Stith
Cover fonts: Montserrat, Marthin Slant
Body copy set in: Crimson Text and F25 Executive

DEDICATED TO

Florence Fern Austin-Wallace's children,

her grandchildren,

her great grandchildren,

and to the generations beyond

INTRODUCTION
BY GARY WALLACE

Our Mother: Her Legacy and My Heritage

As the fifth of seven children I came a little late to the family, but not without fanfare, as I came hungry and would not stop crying until well fed. The same night I was born, my Uncle Paul died in the same home. The doctor had come from a town several miles away to deliver me and stayed on to tend to Uncle Paul until he passed. However, my mother had been taking care of Uncle Paul up until that point, and he had unwittingly infected my mother with tuberculosis before his death. He also infected my two older twin brothers. So began the saga of our lives.

This story is really about the interaction of my mother with her God. At the time she began writing her poems (late 1920's-early 1930's), there were no known drugs or procedures to treat tuberculosis except for prolonged rest, heavy doses of calcium-laden foods, and isolation. Skin tests would show if a person was positive or negative as to being contagious. If one was found to be positive, the "cure" was to go to a sanatorium—away from friends, family, and home. Patients would stay in dormitories with areas that were open to the fresh air and cots or beds were lined up to face the outdoors. For patients ill with tuberculosis, the duration of sanatorium stays was open-ended. One might stay for months or years, or even until death for some.

After my Uncle Paul passed—the very night of my birth—my mother tested positive and chest x-rays confirmed her tuberculosis diagnosis. This diagnosis mandated that she was to be removed from her children and husband.

My older sister, who had just turned six, and my next older brother were placed at the Children's Farm Home, near Corvallis. My other brothers, the twin boys, were found to be positive for tuberculosis as well. Don was sent to a Portland hospital, but lonliness for his twin brother found both of them in the state-run TB hospital in Salem, and they were soon the darlings of the sanatorium, or "San," as we called it back then. I was sent to stay with a newly-married couple when I was about one year old. My mother was placed on a waiting list for the tuberculosis hospital until a bed was available. This would take a year and a half.

Florence Fern Austin-Wallace was a young mother of twenty-six with six children, four of which were being cared for by others, and the other two were infected with this disease, all caused by her nursing our Uncle Paul during his decline. Guilt and pseudo-guilt were demons that haunted her for years to come. Her refuge was her God.

Having come from a non-Christian home, our eighteen-year old our mother and her older sister were introduced to Jesus, possibly during a revival meeting of some sort. She began to attend a Baptist church and sometime during her early conversion days she had decided she wanted to be a missionary to China. At church she also met her husband-to-be.

A year or so later, she would be married, and children soon came along. Travelling to China to become a missionary was a passion of her heart, but after her children were born, the dream ended—she would never be able to

5

travel abroad. However, she would pass on many of her convictions and doctrines of scripture to her seven children. Her God and Savior, Jesus Christ, became our Savior as well. Were it not for her devotional prayers for her children, they might not have been entered into the Book of Life. This became her heritage of eternal life for them. We are all indebted to those faithful ones who have gone before.

I came to a life-long personal relationship with my Creator and Lord of my life and some seventy-five years later, I look back and marvel that within just two years of our family being reunited after Mom's return home from the sanatorium, this trust in God became not just mine, but my next older brother, Ray's, as well!

Many of the poems have specific context and reasons for her anguish and hope. We have tried to pair the content with the events as best as eighty years of recollections can permit. We were, after all, young children during the early years of her writing. Our Mother passed on to us her trust in God's Word and the communication of prayer with our God.

In these poems you will see through a window of the soul; a life of meditations, prayer, and a keen understanding of the Biblical principle, "let the Word of God dwell in you richly." The "working out of your salvation with fear and trembling" is also portrayed in Florence Fern Austin-Wallace's communion with her Lord and His indwelling Holy Spirit.

EDITOR'S NOTE

A missionary is a person who seeks to go to regions that are greatly lacking in knowledge of God's Word and his saving grace.

My mother did not get to go to China during her lifetime but she can now go to our starving twenty-first century America through her poems. Her life is still witnessing to her great God and Savior, Jesus Christ.

She was set aside in that tuberculosis hospital so God could minister to her, and through her, to our dying world.

My prayer is that this work helps you, dear reader, to know Him and to be transformed by the renewing of your mind. Now unto Him be the power and the glory, now and forevermore.

TIMELINE OF FLORENCE FERN AUSTIN-WALLACE'S EARLY YEARS

JUNE 7, 1929	• Graduates from high school • Works at Oregon School for the Blind in Salem, Oregon
SEPT. 19, 1931	• Marries George W. Wallace
JUNE 23, 1932	• Fernadine is born
SEPT. 26, 1933	• Twins Don & Ron are born
NOV. 22, 1934	• Raymon is born
JAN 10, 1936	• George's adoptive father Samuel dies at Florence F. Austin-Wallace's house
DEC. 27, 1936	• Gary is born • Uncle Paul dies from tuberculosis at Florence's home • Florence and Ron and Don test positive for tuberculosis; placed on a waiting list for the Oregon State Tuberculosis Hospital (OSTH)
APRIL 1937	• Don sent to Doernbecher Children's Hospital in Portland to have fluid removed from his lungs from the tuberculosis
DEC 1937	• Death notice arrives; Florence is afraid to open as she fears Don has died. Instead, George's mother Emma has passed away
EARLY 1938	• Gary is sent to live with another family
SPRING 1938	• Florence is pregnant with 6th child
JULY 31, 1938	• Fernadine and Raymon, almost age 3, sent to live at the Children's Farm Home, Corvallis
AUG 1, 1938	• Florence and twins Ron & Don admitted to OSTH.
NOV. 15, 1938	• Carol is born at the Salem Deaconess Hospital, sent to a church family for care. Carol would not return to her family until she was 5 years old.

SPRING 1940	· Florence returns home with Ron & Don, Gary, Ray, and Fernadine.
MARCH 5, 1941	· Florence relapses · Ron & Don, Fernadine, and Ray are sent to Children's Farm Home again Gary to mother's brother's home
1943-1946	· All family members home again · Carol, age 5, comes home for the first time
EARLY 1946	· Florence is pregnant with seventh child and is advised to abort, refuses abortion
SEPT. 23, 1946	· Wayne is born
EARLY 1947	· Florence returns to OSTH for third time. Children all stay at home, except for baby Wayne, who goes to a foster home.
EARLY 1950	· Florence returns home in time to see daughter Fernadine graduate high school as salutatorian
1951	· Don goes in for lung surgery to repair tuberculosis damage. Graduates from Salem High School
1961-1963	· Florence experiences divorce, attempts suicide, experiences restoration
ABOUT 1965	· Enters workforce with no training
1988	· Went to be with her Lord; rest at last

OREGON STATE TUBERCULOSIS HOSPITAL, 1958

THE DEVOTIONAL POEMS OF
FLORENCE FERN AUSTIN-WALLACE

Let the words of my mouth, and the meditation of my heart, be acceptable in thy sight, O LORD, my strength, and my redeemer.

Psalm 19:14

Victory

1927

"Christ liveth in me." Gal. 2:20

"Christ liveth in me." ...He's my Life, and so
I need not walk where He would not go;
As daily I in this knowledge abide,
Counting my self-life with His crucified,
In resurrection life He reigns within,
And I have His power to conquer sin.

"Christ liveth in me." ....He's my Light always;
Since He's shining within, sin cannot stay;
His brilliance dispels defeat and despair
Lighting up my heart with faith and prayer,
Illuminating with His love anew
The lamp of hope, of peace, and joy, too.

"Christ liveth in me." ...He's the living Word;
Evil speech need not from my lips be heard;
He'd not speak in anger, nor hurtfully...
In His gentleness He can speak through me;
His mouthpiece for His own truth I can be,
And His Spirit directs His work in me.

"Christ liveth in me." ...He's my Sight, and so
His own point of view I can come to know:
His love for sinners...not condemnation...
Whether lost ones, or the heirs of salvation;
Since I see that their need is Himself only,
His heart of compassion beats within me.

"Christ liveth in me." ...He's my Righteousness;
This very thought fills me with joyousness;
He has stooped to dwell in my sinful heart,

To fill every need, never to depart,
To take away fear, to give victory;
The pure Son of God deigns to live in me!

*Gary's note: my mother was a sophomore in
high school when this poem was written.*

My Intercessor
1929

If my hands engage in a sinful deed,
In heaven Jesus is interceding;
Where the wrath of a righteous God is stirred,
He for me is gently pleading,
"Father, forgive when this one fails-
For her My hands were pierced with nails."

My feet walk at times where they should not go,
And the Lord's face is turned away from me,
But at God's right hand Jesus is sitting,
Entreating Him ever so patiently,
"Once more this child has met defeat-
Pardon, behold My bruised feet."

If evil thoughts enter into my mind
And I dwell on them a little while,
Christ quickly turns to His Father and cries,
"Surely this is another denial,
But be not angry-remember how
The thorns pricked hard against My brow."

Whenever I am tempted, and I fall,
And false to My Savior I have been,
Jesus is there interceding for me,
"See, she is sorry for her sin;
Father, for this I bled and died-
Look instead at my wounded side."

Whosoever
January 21, 1931
John 3:16

God gave to the world His only Son
And whosoever believes on Him
That everlasting life will win,
Because he has to Christ been know,
Yes, whosoever does believe
Grace and pardon will receive.

And "whosoever" does not mean
That only those of His chosen race
Shall see the light of Jesus' face,
As from God's Word is plainly seen;
Ah, yes, He came first to the Jew
But He came to save the Gentile, too.

"Whosoever" means both black and white,
And color of red or yellow, too;
God cares not of what race are you!
Both East and West have in His sight
An equal promise, if they only dare
Jesus to trust and God's grace to share.

Either rich, or poor, or strong, or weak—
Each one of you has the same right
From sin to turn unto the Light;
God saves if only His face you seek:
If on the Son you will believe,
Everlasting life you shall receive.

"Whosoever" means any of us
Who, realizing our soul's deep need,
Knowing there's no other way indeed,
Do believe and trust in Jesus.
Oh, if now you only could but see
That it means you, it means me!

Thanks
January 22, 1931

I thank God now for Jesus Christ
Who was crucified for me,
Who bore my sin upon the cross,
Who gave salvation, full and true;
I thank Him for that love divine
Which can transform this life of mine.

I thank Him for that precious blood
Which flowed from Calvary,
That flow has washed away my sin-
'tis held no more against me;
I thank Him for the Gift I hold,
And for this peace and joy untold.

WHY ?   (January 26, 1931)

Why, oh, why do you hesitate,
Standing just without the door?
Can't you hear the voice of the Savior
Entreating you not to wait?
   Why not cast every doubt aside?--
   'Twas for you the Christ was crucified.

Why do you not heed His voice?
Is it because your friends may laugh?
Ah, Christ, who died in your behalf,
Is surely much the wiser choice!
   Though they may laugh and scorn you, too,
   Did not He suffer more for you?

———

Why, lost soul, do you turn away?
Is it because the cost is great?
Oh, accept Him before it is too late!
Worldly pleasures mean much to-day,
   But they are only the devil's snare;
   Can't you discern 'tis his voice there?

Why do you say, "Oh, no, not now"?
The Lord's accepted time is to-day;
But Satan is asking you to delay;
Hearing God's voice, why will you allow
   Your life to be ruined by sin and strife?
   Take now God's gift of eternal life.

You admit you know you are lost,
That Christ for you His life did give,
That He bore your sin that you might live,
Yet you reject Him, at what a cost!
   Can't you see that He is the only Way?
   Why not come and accept Him to-day?
     * * * *

Why?
January 26, 1931

Why, oh, why do you hesitate,
Standing just without the door?
Can't you hear the voice of the Savior
Entreating you not to wait?
Why not cast every doubt aside? -
'Twas for you the Christ was crucified.

Why do you not heed His voice?
Is it because your friends may laugh?
Ah, Christ, who died in your behalf,
Is surely much the wiser choice!
Though they may laugh and scorn you, too,
Did not He suffer more for you?

Why, lost soul, do you turn away?
Is it because the cost is great?
Oh, accept Him before it is too late!
Worldly pleasures mean much to-day,
But they are only the devil's snare;
Can't you discern 'tis his voice there?

Why do you say, "Oh no, not now?"
The Lord's accepted time is to-day,
But Satan is asking you to delay;
Hearing God's voice, why will you allow
Your life to be ruined by sin and strife?
Take now God's gift of eternal life.

You admit you know you are lost,
That Christ for you His life did give,
That He bore your sin that you might live,
Yet you reject Him, at what a cost!
Can't you see that He is the only Way?
Why not come and accept Him to-day?

Ever Present
March 10, 1931

Blessed assurance in sorrow or joy:
O'er mountain top or through valley deep,
Though rugged the pathway, or be it steep,
Naught can this confidence destroy:
Christ is ever with me.

Whene'er my head is bent in sorrow,
And my heart is heavy with untold woe,
Comfort the Savior does then bestow;
From this knowledge courage borrow:
Jesus is there to see.

Though friends may laugh, scorn, and deride,
E'en though they all should turn away,
I can walk serene each day;
With unfailing sympathy, close by my side
The Christ will ever be.

When comes temptation with its test,
From the narrow path my feet to lure
And send me wandering o'er the moor,
In the promise of God I can safely rest:
Strength He'll give to me.

Yes, in His word I can rejoice;
For whatever trouble may befall,
Though in this world I may lose all
Still ever near I hear His voice,
"I will never leave thee."

The Call
March 4, 1931

Ah, joy unspeakable! Peace unknown!
When first I came to God's blessed throne;
Come as a sinner, lost, undone,
To Jesus Christ, His precious Son;
Came in faith, just as a child,
And was to Him then reconciled.

Ah, what boundless gratitude within
That God had forgiven me all my sin,
Had lifted me up from sin and strife
With His promise of everlasting life;
That He had given His Son to die
To save a sinner such as I.

The love that welled up in my heart
Became as much of me as a part,
It brought a desire to work for my King
That I might to Him others bring-
A passionate longing I could not still,
That gave no outlet but to do His will.

And then I heard the dear Lord's call-
He was asking me to give up all,
My home, my friends, and my own land,
To go where He led me by His hand,
To heathen nations far or near,
To unbeknownst lands, or countries drear.

Yes, I heard that insistence call so clear-
How could I leave all I hold dear,
Leave friends and home for a strange land?
Why should God so much demand?
Still deep within my heart I knew
That to my Lord I must me true.

So Lord, I surrender unto thee;
What thou wilt, my work shall be;
I'll carry to distant shores Thy Word,
Where the story of Love is never heard.
And because I heed thy pleading voice,
My raptured heart does anew rejoice.

Prayer
April 13, 1931

My heart was heavy with the burden of sin
And I found no comfort anywhere;
'Twas then I sought the Lord in prayer
And all my misery poured out to Him.
As I plead for mercy and searched for light,
God heard my prayer and opened the way-
The words of a friend then brought me to see
The Savior, who turned my night into day.

And when doubt and fear, which soon arose,
Swept o'er my soul like a fiery dart,
Again prayer soothed my troubled heart-
Trusting the Lord brought sure repose;
And often when Satan tempted me
And with his wiles sought to entice,
Always prayer gave me strength to resist,
And to follow my Savior, at any price.

And my refuge now is still in prayer:
I pray, "Help me, Lord, for Thee to live;"
For each new blessing thanks to Him I give,
With Him all my joys and pleasures share;
Sin comes and takes away my peace,
But prayer cleanses, and restores it, too;
And in sorrow, or failure, or discouragement
'Tis ever prayer that carries me through.

To You
April 14, 1931

Be loyal and true, first of all,
To Jesus, your Savior and friend;
Stand for right whatever may befall,
And to others His glad message send:
Live for Him each hour and day,
What He says, that do and obey.

Yield your will, your heart, and your mind-
And not just a part, but the whole-
To the Lord, and blessing you'll find;
Of your life give Him control
And He your course will guide,
As He walks ever close by your side.

Pray ever for strength to endure
Each temptation, trial, and test;
God's answer to prayer does assure,
But remember He knows what is best;
Ask each day for forgiveness of sin-
Tis granted, anew you begin.

Use every faculty and talent
For the enforcement of God's cause;
To you each one by Him was sent,
So labor not for men's applause,
But say, "The gifts thou has given me,
I will ever use, dear Lord, for Thee."

(The first letter of each verse spells out
B.Y.P.U- Baptist Young People's Union.)

Teach Us To Pray
April 24, 1931

As they asked of the Savior then,
Those disciples of long ago,
This petition, "Teach us to pray,"
Now, too, should we do so;
For, like them, we need to be taught
How to pray just as we ought.

So often we never offer
Thanksgiving to God above
For the blessings He bestows,
For His wondrous, infinite love,
Or praise Him for that blessed One
Who died for us-His precious Son.

So often we are too selfish,
Asking only for personal gain,
Not seeking to advance His cause,
Then we grumble, that prayer is in vain.
We ought rather to say with His Son,
"Not my will, but Thine, be done."

So often we make prayer a duty,
Just a task to hurry through,
When we ought to count it a pleasure,
A comfort and a privilege, too,
To share with Him each joy and care,
Knowing He hears our every prayer.

Let us seek to pray aright,
To the Savior's words give heed,
Not asking for what we want,
But trusting Him for what we need;
With the disciples, let us say
To the Lord, "Oh, teach us to pray!"

Cooperation
1937
Mt. 9:37

"The harvest truly is plenteous,
But the laborers are few;"
If you and I have not been called
The actual work to do,
By praying the Lord of the harvest
For the workers in the fields,
And by giving, we, too, may have a part
In the sheaves the harvest yields.

God Is Love
1937
1 John 4:8, 16

"God is love," for when He saw
The deep need of my soul,
Bent beneath its load of sin,
He came to make me whole;
He sent His Son to die for me
Upon the cross of Calvary.

"God is love," and when I feel
The searing breath of pain,
In distress I try to see
The good which I should gain;
It eases suffering to know
That He sees fit to have it so.

"God is love," and each new trial
Through which I'm called to go
Comes but from the Lord in love;
He cares for me, and so
In every trouble on life's way
He is my comfort and my stay.

*Gary's note: Written while waiting for call from
Oregon State Tuberculosis Hospital.*

It Ought To Make A Difference
1937

It ought to make a difference
When we hear Christ say
That He is coming back again-
Suppose that it were today!

It ought to make a difference
In the company we seek;
It ought to make a difference
In every word we speak.

It ought to make a difference
In our daily round of life-
Would we have Him at His coming
Find it filled with sins, or strife?

It ought to make a difference
In choosing things we read,
For that is sure to influence
Our every thought, and deed.

It ought to make a difference
In the talents we invest
In the service of our Savior-
Would He find we give our best?

It ought to make a difference
In each task we have to do,
That we attempt to do it well-

He may come ere we are through.

It ought to make a difference,
Give more incentive to pray -
Surely He'd be pleased to find us
Spending precious time that way.
Lest He should find us shirking.

It ought to make a difference-
And the difference should be
In more holy, righteous living
And in working ceaselessly.

My Faith
1937

What is "great faith?" I do not know;
They tell me that I have it, yet;
Ashamed am I to have it said;
I cannot readily forget
The secret doubtings of my heart,
The times when faith seems to depart.

For when I look down deep within,
My very soul, as God can see,
I find sometimes my faith assailed
By storms of doubt that threaten me
With shipwreck on a foreign shore
Of hopelessness forevermore
A moment thus-God stills the storm;
My wavering faith He brings to rest
In the harbor of His love and grace;
All past experience attest
The wisdom of One who cannot make
One single error or mistake.

Great faith? Ah, no, but a great God
On which to tie my every hope,
A God of love, faithful and true,
One who can successfully cope
With sin, and One who can impart
Perfect faith to a needy heart.

One Day with Christ
1937

Morning-as I from sleep awake,
Into my consciousness there creeps
The joy of knowing Christ the Lord.
I slip from bed my trust to keep
With Him, before the rest arise;
He speaks to me from out His Word,
And seems to be so very near
I find my heart is greatly stirred;
Then on my knees in humble prayer
For guidance through this day I ask,
For grace to triumph over sin,
For strength to meet each daily task.

Noon-day-and He is with me still,
Filling my heart with joy and love;
Tasks and toil are lighter to bear
Because my thoughts are fixed above;
Problems and cares of daily life
Fail long to irk or worry me-
The peace that reigns within my heart
Is not destroyed thus easily.
There comes an opportunity
To one unsaved Christ to present-
I pray the story of love I tell
Perchance may bring him to repent.

Evening-and He has walked with me.
From morn till the hour of setting sun;

I'm sure, as dark comes on apace,
That He will stay till night is done.
We gather for our worship time
Before the children go to rest-
I render thanks to God because
He has this day richly blest.
And as I, too, go to retire,
I feel His presence yet with me;
As Christ was with me all this day,
He'll be with me eternally!

Fear Not
Sept. 22, 1937
Mark 4:40

"Why are ye so fearful?" He asks,
Who stilled the storm in days of yore
Asks it of us here on earth today-
"Why do ye not trust Me more?"

'Tis time our faith is very weak-
Why do we so often feel dismay?
The Savior who bought us with His blood
Surely will care for us alway.

Our hearts grow cold and faint within
When we find ourselves in direst need;
Yet "the earth is the Lord's and the fulness
thereof,"
Surely He can His children feed!

When our souls are laden with sore distress
And despair gives us a heavy heart,
If we take our burden to Him in prayer,
Peace and comfort He will impart.

We pray to our God, "Thy will be done,"
And yet we murmur and question His way;
But surely His wisdom is greater than ours-
He knows best-let's trust Him each day.

Lord, strengthen our faith in thee-our God;

Remove from us all doubts and fears;
We commit ourselves to thy loving hands-
May we trust thee fully in coming years.

I PRAYED   (Oct. 20, 1937)

I prayed - such was my need,
That I could scarcely see
How even Thou could answer, Lord,
And grant that plea for me.

I prayed - and faith Thou gave--
Came the answer from above,
"God shall surely supply your need,
From out His heart of love."

I prayed - and the answer came;
Even as I raised my cry,
Thou had touched the heart of friends
very needs to supply.

O Lord, how can I thank Thee?
I hear Thy answer clear,
"Trust; when thou ask of ME,
I will answer - never fear!"

37

I Prayed
Oct. 20, 1937

I prayed-such was my need
That I could scarcely see
How even God could answer
And grant that plea for me.

I prayed-and faith He gave;
He promised from above,
"God shall surely supply your need
From out His heart of love."

I prayed-and the answer came;
Just as I raised my cry,
God had touched the heart of someone
That very need to supply.

O Lord, how can I thank Thee?
I hear Thy answer clear;
"Just trust when you ask of Me,
I will answer, never fear!"

*Gary's note: This need is, no doubt to placing
her five children, ages 1 through 5 into
acceptable homes as she must go soon to the TB
hospital for undetermined duration. TB was
mostly incurable in those days. And to top it off
she would have her sixth child in the hospital
and would not care for that baby girl until the
child was six years old.*

Enable Me
October 21, 1937

Lord, now myself to thee I yield;
Keep every word that does proceed
From my lips, and each thought and deed,
That I an influence may wield
For good, for truth, and for the right
That I may point lost souls to Thee,
Turn them from darkness to the Light,
That they may be from sin set free.

Keep every word - that I may speak
Nothing to dishonor Thee;
Let me talk of Thee so lovingly
That all will want my God to seek.
And keep my heart and mind so clean,
Set my thoughts on things above,
That a light on my face may be seen,
Revealing to others the indwelling Love.

And if Thou keep each word and thought,
My actions must be in accord;
This is what I seek, O Lord:
To be ever true to Thee who bought
Me with thy blood on Calvary;
To live for Thee each hour and day,
Seeking to win the lost for Thee,
Who are the true and living Way.

Good to Know
November 15, 1937

It's good to know that God is near
When life seems dismal, dark, and drear,
To know that I am never alone-
His comforting arms around me thrown,
Strengthening, aiding, sustaining me
In this trying storm upon life's sea.

When my burden seems more than I can bear
'Tis good to know He hears my prayer;
It eases the heartache, and the fear
That greater trouble may appear,
Assures me the Lord does all things well,
And the comfort it brings no tongue can tell.

Now when my heart is near despair,
It's good to cast my every care
On Him who's promised to care for me;
Trusting Him fully and utterly
Brings comfort amid this trial and test,
And even joy, and peace and rest.

Without Question
November 16, 1937

Why this new trial, why, oh, why?
O Lord, give ear unto my cry!
Had not I enough of regret and woe?
Why continue thou to afflict me so?
Why add to my fear for ones I love?
I seek the reason, O God above.

Can this burden that thou hast sent
Be for me more chastisement
For failing thee in days gone by?
Could this be the reason why?
If that is why I've trouble yet,
'Tis a lesson I'll not soon forget.

Or is it true that this may be
Just to test my faith in thee?
If such be so, may I not fail
To stand the test -may it avail
To draw one to thee closer still,
Submissive always to thy will.

Does it matter so much after all
Why my trouble should befall?
I have no right to question thee,
Whatever comes to mine, or me,
Thou hast a reason, O Lord above,
I'll trust thy everlasting love.

I Need Thee
November 21, 1937

I need Thee so much, O Lord,
More now than ever before;
Be Thou very near to me—
Forsake me not, I implore,
In this time of deep distress,
When cares and fears oppress.

I need Thee to give me strength
To meet each coming day
With a calm and serene heart,
Trusting in Thee always
To drive away my every fear
Tho the way seem dark and drear.

I need Thee to keep me true
When I am tempted to stray
Away from my Savior's side,
Forsaking the right way;
In temptation, Lord, teach me
I must rely alone on Thee.

I need Thee to lift me up
When I am near despair
O'er mistakes past and gone;
Then to my knees in prayer
Send me, Lord—'tis a remedy
That never fails to uphold me.

O Lord, my every deep need
Thou hast promised to supply:
Give me new strength and courage,
As the days go passing by;
And keep one ever close to Thee,
Here from fear and worry free.

One Hour of Worship
November 28, 1937

That privilege was mine
To be in God's house today,
To worship and to sing His praise
After some time away;
And to join with others there
In the sweet fellowship of prayer.

My heart was filled with joy
As we raised our voices in song
And the rapture of those moments
Has been with me all day long;
For the hymns we there were singing
Still within my heart are ringing.

There as we bowed our heads
And lifted heart and voice
In prayer to our Redeemer,
Then again did I rejoice;
I could feel the very essence
Of the Savior's divine presence.

As I listened to our pastor
Give the message of the morn,
New resolve to serve God better
Within my heart was born.
So deeply sank that sermon heard
It seemed indeed to be God's Word.

Something in the fellowship
During such a sacred hour
Draws me closer to my Savior,
Makes me conscious of His power,
And the blessing I had come to seek
Goes with me throughout the week.

*Gary's note: probably the first time I attended
First Baptist Church (5th & Lyon Street, Albany,
Oregon) at 11 months old.*

A Prayer for Today
October 4, 1938

Lord, help me to live just for today,
Not a vain regret for yesterday,
Facing tomorrow without a fear,
Secure in the knowledge Thou art near.

Help me to see, as the day goes by,
There is no time for a tear or sigh;
By gleaning the best from each new hour,
True happiness lies within my power.

Help me to do the little I can
To cheer the heart of the fellow-man;
Perhaps just a kindly word or a smile,
And someone may find that life's worthwhile.

Still give me a song within my heart
Even though the joys of life depart;
May I find a greater joy in Thee
And in thy service, this is my plea.

Through all this day, O Lord, keep me
Free from indulging in self-pity;
May I remember Thou knowest best,
Whatever the trial or the test.

When there comes the end of day,
Grant that I may be able to say
In my inmost heart, "I am content,"
Because this day for Thee was spent.

Gary's note: Her first poem after entering OSTH.

Patience

1938

So often I prayed for patience,
And yet I failed to see
That I had made much progress
Toward what I long to be.

For only trouble and heartache
And trials come my way,
Till I had need of patience
To bear them day by day.

"Tribulation worketh patience,"
Thus does God's Word declare,
So perhaps this tribulation
Is answer to my prayer!

Loneliness
Summer 1938

(Gary, gone to a foster home at about one year
old)
Loneliness...
I never knew before
The value of my baby's
Fond caress.

(Fernadine, gone to the Children's Farm Home.)
How I miss
My little daughter's voice
In eagerness and questioning,
And her kiss.

(Raymon, gone to the Children's Farm Home.)
Shy, yet bold,
"I like you 'muvver," he would say,
That sturdy little man of mine,
Three years old.

(Don and Ron, gone to OSTH for several months.)
Gone so long,
Yet still I miss them so,
My two lads of five...
Lord, make me strong!

Too Tired To Pray
1938

Lord, I am too weary-
I will not pray tonight
"How else can your spirit
Be strengthened for the fight?"
But, Lord, I am <u>so</u> tired,
And a bit distressed.
"Prayer will soothe your heartache,
And give your body rest."

O Lord, my thoughts are blurred-
I cannot pray tonight!
"Dear child, the Holy Spirit
Will help you pray aright."
But, Lord, I am so worn
I do not <u>want</u> to pray.
"Ah, child, what better reason
To seek Me right away?

Lord, I now am kneeling-
Yes, I will heed Thy voice;
And here now in Thy presence
I cannot but rejoice.
Forgive me, Lord, for faltering-
The truth Thy words expressed:
"Come unto Me, ye weary,
And I will give you rest."

He Upholds
Jan. 8, 1938
Proverbs 24:10

One day I was worried and sad,
Depressed, discouraged in heart,
When one verse from out of God's Word
In my thoughts came to stand apart.

I know 'twas the Lord who sent it-
I was not conscious that I knew
That little passage of Scripture,
Until into my mind it flew.

"If thou faint in the day of adversity,
Thy strength is small indeed-
How is it brought to me just the message
Of which I was most in need!

To the faith that I have in God
Surely all my strength is tied:
The depth of my trust in the Lord
Strength or weakness must decide.

I saw I must never allow
My faith to become too small,
As I walk the pathway of life,
Lest, weary and faint, I should fall.

What rebuke, what shame it brought me!
And I went to the Lord in prayer

To ask His pardon for doubting
My Savior's love and His care.

As always, prayer brought peace;
And when that day I recall,
It brings me new assurance
He will never let me fall.

My Light
January 13, 1938

"Ye are the light of the world"-
Lord, make my ray to shine
Brightly, clearly, incessantly,
Revealing Thy light divine.

But I must be a burning light,
If I would brighten the gloom;
All selfish desire and appetite
The fire must consume,

'Till all the dross has vanished
And only the gold remains,
And a purified personality
To the world Thy light proclaims.

O Thou incarnate Light,
Grant that others may see
In my borrowed ray a clear,
Tho faint, reflection of Thee.

O living Light within my heart,
Set my soul aflame
With a passion for aiding others
The Light of Life to claim.

"A burning and a shining light,"
Dear Lord, make me to be,
Glowing each day brighter,
Lighting the way to Thee.

My Record
Jan. 20, 1938

I slept, and dreamed I looked upon
A book with pages only three,
Wherein I read, and saw inscribed
A record which God keeps of me-
The first page black, next red, then white,
Each one in turn before my sight.

On the black leaf I saw these words:
"The soul that sinneth, it shall die;"
Beneath, "the wages of sin is death"
And "all have sinned" I did decry;
Then in despair I made this plea,
"O God, be merciful to me!"

That page was turned, the red displayed:
"He was bruised for our iniquities,"
"We have redemption through His blood,"
"Christ died for us"-thus God decrees;
Then faith came, as I heard Him say
These words of Life, "I am the Way."

And quickly that leaf, too, was turned,
A page of glistening white to show,
And written there in letters clear,
"Your sins...shall be as white as snow;"
Christ's blood has washed and made me whole,
Forever cleansed my guilty soul!

"Come Unto Me"
(to an unsaved sister) February 18, 1938

"Come unto ME", Jesus is saying -
Hark to the sound of His pleading voice;
"You who are wearied and saddened by life,
Come unto ME, and make ME your choice."

"Come unto ME" - He loved you enough
To go to the Cross and die in your place;
The perfect One suffered there for your sins,
Just to save from shame and disgrace.

"Come unto ME" - can you not see Him,
Waiting with arms open wide to receive,
Weeping because you have waited so long?
Why do you longer His loving heart grieve?

"Come unto ME" - the loved ones departed,
In Heaven, are waiting your coming some day;
Vain is their hope unless you will listen
To Jesus' own words of "I am the Way."

"Come unto ME"-you owed it to those
Whom God has entrusted into your hands;
You can only mold those lives aright
By turning to Christ, as duty demands.

"Come unto ME" - dare you reject Him?
Remember the Judgement coming some day;
Time may be short - decide now your fate,

And come to the Savior while you may.

"Come unto ME" - perfect solution
For all of your trials, all of your grief;
If you come unto Jesus, a perfect peace
Will enter your heart and bring relief.

Trust in Trial
April 13, 1938

This seems one trial too much,
Hope is well nigh dead,
Despair threatens to crush me,
All my courage has fled;
Peace has left my heart–
Rebellion reigns instead.

Still a voice faintly whispers–
Through a darkness a ray
Of consolation appears–
Surely this is God's way;
It is His hand that sends it,
So I can only pray.
"Lord, give me needed vision
In this to see Thy hand,
On Thy promises to me
Now teach me, Lord to stand,
Humbly trusting Thee although
I cannot understand."

Somehow my heart is lighter

After lifting that prayer,

New hope and strength come surging

Only because I dare

Just to trust God's way for me,

His watchful, loving care.

Gary's note: she found herself to be pregnant with her sixth child while still waiting for a bed to open up at OSTH.

To An Old Lady
March 21, 1938

Alone? "Yes! And so sad, so lonely,
With just myself for company only;
Husband now gone, and children away,
Hours drag miserably day by day,
Friends come seldom to lessen the gloom
Of living alone in my little room?

Alone? Ah no! do you forget
There is One who's with you yet,
Close by your side and ready to cheer
Your loneliness, One ever near
To lighten each day so weary grown?
The child of God is never alone!

Do you often turn, comfort to seek,
To God's Word, and let Him speak
Consolation to your aching heart?
Do you not find in every part
Assurance of His presence with you
That ever brings rejoicing anew?

Do you remember God's love and care?
Do you often kneel in prayer?
Just ask of Him in confidence
To give you the evidence
That He is near, and this He'll do—
He'll make His presence real to you.

Peace
Sept. 1938

That peace past understanding
I never knew until
God sent the roaring breakers,
And then said, "Peace, be still!"

He gives me abiding peace
In place of fear and dread;
For pleasures He took away
He gives His joy instead.

For the ceaseless ache of heart
He whispers unto me:
"I would not send thee ought
But what is good for thee."

For the long hours of loneliness
I have His promise sure,
That He will never leave me
Through all I must endure.

From worry over my loved ones
His dear voice sets me free:
"I know what is best for them
As surely as for thee."

Can I wish the waves of trial
Had never come my way?
The peace He has given is worth
More than He took away.

What Will You Do?
Nov. 11, 1938

If you do not know the Lord,
Dear Friend, what will you do
If sorrow which comes to all,
Should sometime come to you?

What if earthly friends forsake,
As they so often do,
If you do not know that Friend
Who will not forsake you?

What will you do when trials
Come and make life dreary,
If you cannot trust in His word,
"My grace is sufficient for thee?"

When problems come to baffle
And there seems nowhere to turn,
Then what will you do, my friend,
If you the Savior spurn?

If you shun the way of Life
And treat Jesus shamefully,
What will you do as death nears
And you face eternity?

Now don't you think it wisest
To come and acknowledge your need
Of the Savior who died for you?

Won't you this message heed?

Gary's note: Written four days before she gave birth to her sixth child at the Salem Deaconess Hospital.

Divine Comfort

December 31, 1938
"He healeth the broken in heart, and bindeth up
their wounds." Psalms 147:3

Though the world is filled with sorrow,
"He heals the broken in heart,"
Lifts the curtain drawn over each woe,
Bidding the night depart.
How real the compassionate Christ
When comes grief or disease;
Only the hand of a loving God
Can bind such wounds as these.

Bitterness attendant with sorrow
Melts at the touch of His hand,
At the depth of tenderness in His voice,
"Your pathway I have planned."
All the deep, unending heartbreak
God can soothe, and loving is He,
For there flows from His heart of love
Rich streams of sympathy.

Midst the gloom of disappointed hopes,
The despair of an aching heart,
His gracious design may be to teach
The comfort He can impart;
Human sympathy cannot reach
To the depths of a woe untold,
But our hearts adoringly echo
Those words of the psalmist of old.

Self-Questioning
December 9, 1938

Is it pleasing to God,
This thing I do?
Shall I cease from it,
Or see it through?
What value is there in it for me?
Will it truly add to God's glory?
Or is it a whim,
A fancy that has no lasting good?
Must the voice of conscience be understood?
Or does it please Him?

Are they pleasing to God,
These words as I speak?
Or idle and foolish,
Meaningless, weak?
Will they reflect to anyone's hurt?
Are they wrathful, rancorous, or curt?
Or do they behoove
One who professes to know the Lord?
Will they later be sadly deplored?
Or does He approve?

Heaven
1939

Sometimes I long for heaven,
That place of perfect bliss
In the presence of the Almighty God;
Surely it is not amiss
To wish to meet Him face to face
In that eternal dwelling-place.

"The Lamb is the light thereof,"
"There shall be no night there,"
No night of sorrow or crying,
No blackness or despair,"
The glory of God will be the light
That dispels all darkness of the night.

"And there shall be no more pain"
Of body nor ache of the heart;
Cessation from suffering comes
When we this life depart;
Gone, too, our foolish doubts and fears,
"And God shall wipe away all tears!"

Death of this mortal body
Can hold no fear for me-
"There shall be no more death"
Through all eternity,
We'll ask, "O death, where is thy sting?"
It will only life eternal bring!

"And His servants shall serve Him,"
Not weakly serve, as now,
Then humbly in perfect worship
And adoration bow;
And through the ages we shall sing
Praises to our Savior King.

"And they shall see His face,"
All those for whom He died,
Look on the Lord of glory,
The Lamb once crucified;
Ah, heaven's greatest joy will be
To see His face who died for me!

I Am Content
1939

"I have learned in whatsoever state I am,
therewith to be content." Phil. 4:11

I think I've learned to be content
Where'er, however my days are spent,
For "as Thou wilt" is now the song
My heart is singing all day long.

Why should I long for riches, wealth?
He gives me of His precious self;
My need He's promised to supply—
What cause for discontent have I?

Though trials fall across my way,
I'll thank Him while it is today
For blessings that the trials hold—
I am repaid one hundred fold!

And when sometimes His face grows dim
He gives me strength to trust in Him,
To walk by faith and not by sight,
'Till once again "I am the light."

When weak in body, or in pain,
I have no reason to complain;
I can rejoice that He knows best;
His blessing hides in every test.

When my lonely heart often aches,
He stands beside me here and takes
On Himself my anguish and grief,
And thus He brings to me relief.

Whene'er the path of life is rough,
I always find my Lord enough,
That my every need He can fill-
I rest contented in His will.

Murmur Not

1939

"Neither murmur ye." (1 Corinthians 10:10)

Help me not to murmur, Lord,
Only to see Thy hand
In every situation;
And know that Thou has planned
For my own good in everything;
In each trying matter
That I am called upon to face,
And when great trials shatter
The heart's fondest ambitions
With one full sweeping blow,
Or in each trifling burden
Thou art all-wise and know
That I have need of these-
It's thus I grow in grace,
Blossom under discipline,
And learn to give first place
Unto my Savior and my God,
To live as unto Thee.
So keep me, Lord, from murmuring,
Whatever comes to me!

Prayer Changes Things
1939

It changes the monotony
Of this daily life of mine
Into the opportunity
To serve my Lord divine;
It changes tasks and toiling
That so irksome were before
Into duties of delight,
As I seek to please Him more.

It eases the little heartaches
Just to tell them to the Lord,
Sure that He cares, yet knowing they
With His will are in accord;
And even in greater sorrows
There I find a refuge sweet,
Drawn away from the multitude,
Kneeling down at Jesus' feet.

When reading His blessed Word,
I ask the Lord to impart
Some truth, and He illumines
And applies it to my heart;
And whenever there's the burden
That an unconfessed sin gives,
The moment that I ask Him,
I find that He forgives.

If bitterness creeps o'er me

At some real or fancied wrong,
As I plead for love before Him
All my malice melts ere long;
I pray for strength to conquer,
From each fault to be made free;
And I have found a precious truth;
Best of all, prayer changes <u>me.</u>

Sufficiency

1939

"Because of his importunity, he will...give him
as many as he needeth." Luke 11: 8

As much food as we need
For our daily bread;
With as much as we need
Each day we'll be fed;
But how much is our need
The Lord must decide;
Food for body and soul
And God will provide

As much strength as we need
To hear weal or woe,
As much strength as we need
To vanquish the foe,
As much strength as we need
To finish each task-
This strength He will give
To us, if we ask.

As much faith as we need
In His Word to trust,
As much faith as we need
To live as we must,
As much fath as we need
To drive away fear,
Perfect faith He will give
To make our way clear.

As much love as we need
All things to endure,
As much love as we need
To keep our lives pure.
As much love as we need
By His plan to live,
Love for God and for man—
This love He will give.

And food for the body
And food for the soul,
For the strength that we need
To attain our goal,
For faith in His power,
A heart filled with love,
We must just importune
Our Father above.

White Unto Harvest
1939
Mt. 9:37

"The harvest truly is plenteous,
But the laborers are few,"
If you and I have not been called
The actual work to do,
By praying the Lord of the harvest
For the workers in the fields,
And by giving, we, too, may have a part
In the sheaves the harvest yields.

Without Christ

1939

"Without me, ye can do nothing." John 15:2

"Without Me, you can do nothing-
Listen to Me as I speak,
O child with spirit that's willing,
But flesh that is strangely weak.

"Without me, you can do nothing-
Alone you cannot attain
A life that is pleasing to Me;
Without me, striving is vain.

"Without Me, you can do nothing-
Except you seek Me in prayer,
You cannot be free from your sin:
That comes through fellowship there.

"Without Me, you can do nothing-
Unless you follow the voice
Of conscience, wherein I speak,
How can you hope to rejoice?

"Without Me, you can do nothing-
But can I prosper and bless
The plans that you make without Me,
When no need of Me you confess?

"Without Me, you can do nothing-
Are you trusting Me to guide,

When rebellion fills your heart
Over things you are denied?

"Without Me, you can do nothing-
Don't leave Me out of your life,
I am able to guide and keep you
From all sin and constant strife.

"Without Me, you can do nothing-
But if in Me you abide,
Then I can give you victory
Whatever there may betide.

"Without Me, you can do nothing."
Oh, my Lord, with heart contrite,
I bow and ask forgiveness,
Ask that You will keep me right.

Jan 17, 1939

Walls

Sometimes I feel surrounded
By lofty walls on every hand,
Walls I cannot see beyond—
I'm captive in a stormy land,
Distressed by winds of trial,
Swept by hurricanes of doubt,
Shut away from trust and hope
And the joy and peace without.

Behind is a wall of failure,
An ugly wall of past mistakes—
The record embroidered of all my sin
This wall of depression makes.
If I turn to left or right,
Nearby stands a wall of fear;
The awful fear of what may come
Unto those that I hold dear.

So closely joined to those of fear,
And worst of all confronting me,
Looms large another awful wall,
A wall of dread uncertainty;
Could I only look beyond
That wall, there the future see,
I think it would help me to meet
Good or ill, whichever it be.

But when I lift my eyes on high,
There is the Lord I am aware
The wall of sin has disappeared,
Only a Cross is standing there;
The walls of fear have crumbled—
The presence of God sets free;
And He knows all the future—
What blessed security!

Walls
January 17, 1939

Sometimes I feel surrounded
By lofty walls on every hand,
Walls I cannot see beyond-
I'm captive in a stormy land,
Distressed by winds of trial,
Swept by hurricanes of doubt,
Shut away from trust and hope
And the joy and peace without.

Behind is a wall of failure,
An ugly wall of past mistakes-
The remembrances of all my sin
This wall of depression makes.
If I turn to the left or right,
Nearby stands a wall of fear,
The awful fear of what may come
To those that I hold dear.

So closely joined to those of fear,
And worst of all confronting me,
Loomed large another awful wall,
A wall of dread uncertainty;
Could I only look beyond
That wall, there the future see,
I think it would help me to meet
The good or ill, which'er it be.

But when I lift my eyes on high,

There is the Lord-I am aware
The wall of sin has disappeared,
Only a cross is standing there;
The walls of fear have crumbled-
The presence of God sets free;
And He knows all the future-
What a blessed security!

*Gary's note: Must have been written regarding
the losses of family and their futures-who/how
will those I love be? Her prayers to a faithful
God! I am living testimony to those prayers as
are all my siblings....*

The Creator
January 19, 1939

Blest indeed is one who sees
God in flowers and birds and trees;
In grass and hills, in woods and sky,
And in majestic mountains high;
In rushing rivers, tiny streams;
In moonlight, in a star that gleams;
In gentle breeze or mighty gale,
In falling rain, or snow, or hail;
In orchards blossoming in Spring,
A flight of wild geese on the wing;
In harvest fields of golden grain,
The barren beauty of a plain;
In sand upon the ocean shore,
That ocean with its ceaseless roar.

Could one ask for a greater bliss
Than to enjoy a world like this?
Yet God, who made the beauty we see
All about us constantly,
Who out of nothing could create
A world so beautiful and great,
Can take an ugly, sin-scarred soul,
And by His grace can make it whole;
God, out of chaos and defeat,
Can cleanse that soul and make it meet
To serve Him in a better land,
One so marvelous and so grand
That the beauty of earth will, we'll find,
Not be remembered nor come to mind.

Quietness

January 25, 1939

"He giveth quietness." Job 24:29a

I sought a manifestation
In this fiery ordeal,
Some evidence of God's love,
Something I could feel;
But to me no sign was granted...
The Lord could see I must
Learn a very precious lesson:
In His Word alone to trust.

So amid the seething turmoil
To His promises I turned...
They were all the comfort left me,
And my lesson well I learned!
Then there came a quietude
I cannot well express,
A steady calmness of the heart...
"He giveth quietness."

It is quietness that comes
From believing in my God
And in His surpassing love;
He will take away the rod
When His design is served,
And I have learned it pays
To make more of life for God,
To bear witness to His praise.

The Word of Life

Jan. 27, 1939

"Holding forth the Word of life." Phil. 2: 16

Hold forth the Word of life
To the many deep in need
Of a living Savior;
Keep sowing precious seed—
It may take root and grow,
Some soul to Christ may lead.

Hold forth the Word of life—
He has promised faithfully
It shall not void return,
And it is the only key
To unlock a strong heart
That is given you and me.

Hold forth the Word of life
To each sinful, dying one—
Tell again the story
Of the Lord who sent His son
To save that soul from death,
Tell it o'er till life is done.

Hold forth the Word of life,
Preach the love of Christ the Lord,
How this loving Savior
On the cross His life out-poured;
Souls lost by your silence
God cannot well afford.

Hold forth the Word of life-
Your assured reward shall see
In the joy of service here,
As you witness faithfully;
Reward in heaven will
A crown of rejoicing be.

I Pray
February 9, 1939

I know the secret of happiness,
The God-appointed way
To make life's day more beautiful-
'Tis only that I PRAY.

I pray in trouble and trial-
These cannot take away
The inner peace and joy
God gives me when I PRAY.

Prayer keeps the fires of faith
Burning brightly each day;
I cannot please God without faith-
More reason that I PRAY.

Prayer destroys desire for rubbish
That would clutter my way;
The Christ-life within is nourished,
As trustingly I PRAY.

Prayer keeps a person happy;
In prayer my spirit may
Have communion with my Lord-
And that is why I PRAY.

Teach Me
Feb. 10, 1938

I need a lesson in patience, Lord-
It seems sometimes the very thing
I try so much to guard against
Irritation and vexation bring.

I need a lesson in forgiveness-
"Until seventy times seven" so You say,
And though I quickly seek to forget,
Resentment comes along to stay.

Lord, perhaps what I need is a lesson
In trusting Thy power to keep me free
From the sin which doth so easily beset,
Letting increased faith win the victory.

Teach me a perfect submission, Lord;
Teach me patiently my trials to bear;
So fill my heart with Thy joy and love
That there'll be no room for evil there.

Rejoicing
February 14, 1939

Lord, even here on a sick-bed,
Days are not tiresome or long;
Thou art ever here beside me
To fill my heart with a song,
A song of rejoicing and trust,
A song of Thanksgiving to Thee
For the many God-given joys
And blessings remaining to me.

There is joy just in the saying,
"Not my will, but Thine, be done,"
In trusting my all to the wisdom
Of the great omniscient One;
Though sometimes it may be painful,
I will wait submissive and still,
Till Thou hast perfected in me
The work of Thy gracious will.

There is joy in testifying
To Thy wondrous saving grace;
Since Thou hast placed me here,
I seek not a better place;
Guided by Thy Holy Spirit,
May I witness faithfully...
Lord, use me here to lead
Christ-less souls to turn to Thee.

There is joy wherever Thou art,

And with me Thou wilt ever be;
I have never a cause for distress...
Thy grace is enough for me.
So keep me joyfully trusting,
Content to leave always to Thee
The charting of my course
Throughout life and eternity.

The Call
February 16, 1939

Have you heard the call of Christ?
"Not called," I hear you say...
Rather, you have not heeded,
Have only turned away.

Have you daily looked within
The pages of God's Word,
Seen man's lost estate, and still
The call you have not heard?

Have you not heard the call?
"Go ye," our Savior said;
And yet perhaps you never
One soul to Him have led.

Can't you hear the bitter cry
Of burdened hearts in sin,
Longing for peace and pardon?
Seek you their souls to win?

When you look upon men's sorrows,
The aching hearts and sore,
You who know God's comfort,
Can you their grief ignore?

Do you not sense the longing
In every human heart?
To aid in their search for God
Are you doing your part?

Joy In Sorrow

February 22, 1939

"Sorrow is turned into joy before Him." Job
41:22

In deep, heartbreaking sorrow,
With the Lord brought face to face,
Still we know He is effecting
In our lives a work of grace;
In the hour of disappointment,
Through our eyes with tears are dim,
All our mourning turns to gladness,
As in faith we bow to Him.

In the presence of the Lord,
Although darkness clouds the skies,
We discern that all our trials
Are His "mercies in disguise;"
We know and love the Hand
That permits our every grief-
He who allows the wound alone
Can administer relief.

In each sorrow there remains
Before Him a peace serene,
Blossoming to buoyant gladness
As upon His arms we lean;
Deepest sorrow only brings us
To exultant joy at length,
And in weakness we can make
The joy of the Lord our strength.

Send Me
February 23, 1939

"Here I am, Send me." Is. 6:8

Lord, here am I, a lowly sinner,
But a sinner saved by Thy grace;
Here am I, ready and waiting
For Thou to use me any place;
Here am I, helpless without Thee...
Give of Thy strength, for I am weak;
Here am I, so slow of tongue...
Supply the words with which to speak.

Lord, here am I, lacking in meekness,
So full of pride and vanity...
Cleanse me from these secret faults,
And clothe me with humility;
Here am I, much too indifferent
To the value of just one soul...
Instill in me an intense yearning
To see lost sinners saved, made whole.

Lord, send me...even in my weakness,
Thou canst use me in Thine own way;
Lord, send me...not in some future time,
But where I am, use me today;
Just now, just here, with all my failings,
To Thee in faith my life I yield...
Thou canst make me a fruitful worker
In my part of the harvest field.

It Is The Lord
March 8, 1939
"It is the Lord; let Him do what seemeth Him
good." 1 Sam. 3:18

It is God who sends the sunshine
That is ours upon life's way;
It's He who clears the cloudy skies,
Makes bright again the day;
He smooths our paths and blesses
With joy that reaches deep
We have the happy days because
He does them peaceful keep.

Likewise, it is the Lord who brings
Anguish, sorrow, deepest woe,
Each discouragement and trouble,
Disappointment's bitter blow;
The things that fret or grieve us,
The trials, great or small,
The Lord sends-or He permits them-
His hand is in them all.

Let us bow in acquiescence
To the working of His will;
Let Him do as He sees fitting,
We will love and trust Him still;
The end from the beginning
Is hidden from our eyes,
But He sees and works a purpose
That is loving, that is wise.

The Joy of The Lord

March 19, 1939

"The joy of the Lord is your strength." Neh. 8:10

This is the secret of triumph,
The secret of all victory:
He who overcomes is one
In whose heart rings a melody;
It's the joy of the surrendered heart,
Which fully knows God's wondrous grace,
That gives this strength, as of one
Who has met the Lord face to face.

We have no strength of ourselves
When we bow beneath some sorrow,
But our hearts are warmed by His joy,
And from this, strength we borrow;
Responsibilities fail to daunt us,
Sharp words or wrongs cannot annoy,
And duties are turned into delight
By hidden springs of inward joy.

Joy opens the streams of devotion—
We more quickly obey the call
To tell the story of a Savior
And of how He suffered for all;
It impels to action and service,
This glorious joy of the Lord,
And we can only do our best work
In the strength peace and joy afford.

Remembrancers

April 4, 1939

"Ye that are the Lord's remembrancers, keep
not silence." Isaiah 62: 6 (marginal translation)

We are the Lord's "remembrancers"-
What a blessed, solemn thought!
Since He trusts in us with this duty,
How diligently we ought
To give it a foremost place,
Nor relax; even for a space.

Do you sometimes get discouraged
At the sameness of the task?
His command is, "Keep not silence,"
Still continue then to ask
For those upon your prayer list-
Just how many have you missed?

All these patient intercessions
In behalf of others, tend
To bear fruit in our own lives,
And our labor's ultimate end
Will be blessing on them poured,
Which will magnify our Lord.

The Christct of the Cross
April 7, 1939

I prayed once to the Lord,
"Make the Christ upon the cross
More real to me than now;
May His death my soul engross;
Help my finite mind to grasp
More fully what a great price
He paid there just for me,
What a matchless sacrifice."

God heard my prayer, for now
Unspeakably dear to me
Is the vision of my Savior
On the cross of Calvary;
My heart now melts within me,
And my eyes grow blurred and dim;
My love flows out in gratitude
And adoration to Him.

As now I look about me,
There is born a new desire,
For there springs up within
Such a constant, living fire
Of yearning to see the lost
Claim this Christ of Calvary,
That to witness I am constrained
By His very love for me.

Supreme Suffering
April 10, 1939

"Someone has to suffer,"
I heard a woman say,
"Before some lasting good comes,
The price of someone must pay."

Yes, Someone had to suffer-
God saw it must be done
To save a lost humanity;
That someone was His Son.

Someone had to suffer,
Die for your sin and mine-
That Someone must be perfect,
A Man and yet Divine.

Someone had to suffer-
God's love said it must be,
Sent Jesus to His death
On the cursed tree.

Someone had to suffer
To cleanse our hearts within;
For without shedding of blood
There's no pardon for sin.

Someone had to suffer,
Die of a broken heart,
Before God could to us

His salvation impart.

Someone had to suffer-
Has He died for you in vain?
Or will you accept His sacrifice
And your salvation gain?

Reaping
April 16, 1939

"Whatsoever a man soweth,
That shall he also reap"
Is the inescapable law
That for all the world must keep,
A natural and moral law that holds
Alike for sinner and saint,
But a promise is given the Christian,
Lest with remorse he grow faint.

"All things work together for good"
To all those who are His own,
So even though I must reap
For the evil I have sown,
In the midst of the harvest of trials
Resulting from past mistakes,
A wise and loving Father
The trials a blessing makes.

"Thy judgements are righteous, Lord,"
I cry from a contrite heart,
"I know Thou hast chosen for me
In my life a goodly part;
Thou hast stood beside me in trial,
Thou hast blest abundantly -
I thank Thee for the affliction
That draws me closer to Thee!"

Gary's note: Her sin of the past weighs heavy in remorse but faith triumphs over it.

In His Name

"Whatsoever ye shall ask in My name, that will
I do."
John 14:13

Each time I lift a prayer on high,
In Jesus' name I seek to pray,
For the power of prayer depends upon
Using His name in the right way;
The matchless name of Jesus Christ
Becomes an all-sufficient plea
Only as my life shows forth
Just what that name has meant to me.

He can trust me with His interests
If I yield myself to live
Only for Him and for His cause-
Then will He most freely give
Whatever I ask in His name,
All the necessary supplies
For the conduct of His business;
This is where the secret lies.

"Do all in the name of the Lord."
So plainly directs His Word-
As I bear His name before men,
Just so will my prayer be heard;
If I seek not my own but His will,
His nature of love becomes mine,
And the cry of His Spirit within my heart
Is a prayer in His name divine.

The Touch Divine
May 10, 1939

Lord, Thou has touched my heart
And made it new and clean-
Oh, how I love Thee now
And to Thy service lean!

Lord, Thou hast touched my head,
And now I want to think
Thy thoughts after Thee, as Thou
My mind with Thine dost link.

Lord, Thou hast touched my will-
It's no more mine, but Thine;
With joy I walk the way
Thou dost appoint as mine.

Lord, Thou hast touched my eyes-
The beauty now I see
Of holiness and love
That emanate from Thee.

Lord, Thou hast touched my ears
And taught me to revere
The music of Thy voice,
To heed the voice I hear.

Lord, Thou hast touched my hands
And now they work for Thee,
Carrying where'er I go

The Cross of Calvary.

Lord, Thou hast touched my feet
And made them to be shod
With the gospel of Thy peace,
Good tidings sent from God.

I long for greater grace,
O lord with touch divine;
A deeper touch of faith and love
Bring to this life of mine.

Trust
May 17, 1939

He is a God for great needs,
But also for the small;
And to trust Him in small matters
Is the hardest thing of all.
We look for great deliverance
In some threatening hour,
But confronted with a trivial need,
We fail to trust His power.

The God who reared the mountains
And hollowed out the seas
Forms a tiny blade of grass
And brings the gentle breeze;
The God who guides the stars above
Also perfumes the rose
And clothes the lily of the field
And every flower that grows.

O ye of little faith, and slow
To trust your Father's care,
For every need, however small,
Now is the time to dare
To believe what He has said,
And know the sweet release
From care, that brings the trusting heart
Great area of peace.

Neither Murmurs Ye

"Neither murmurs ye." 1 Cor. 10:10

Help me not to murmur, Lord,
Only to see Thy hand
In every situation,
And know that Thou hast planned
For my own good in everything.
In each trying matter
I am called upon to face,
And when great trials shatter
The heart's fondest ambitions
With one fell sweeping blow,
Or in each trifling burden,
Thou art all-wise and know
That I have need of these-
'Tis thus I grow in grace,
Blossom under discipline,
And learn to give first place
Unto my Savior and my Lord,
To live as unto Thee.
So keep me, Lord, from murmuring,
Whatever comes to me!

Today
June 12, 1939

To rightly live this present day
As if my last, and well I may...
For I know not what a day may bring;
To seek God's will in everything;
    This is my goal today.

To scatter cheer along my way;
For loved ones, friends, and self to pray;
Unto the Lord some soul to lead;
To honor Him in word and deed:
    This is my task today.

To yield to Jesus everything;
To make Him Master, Lord, and King;
To use what talents I possess
For Him in service He can bless:
    This is my joy today.

To hear the trump of God resound,
No more upon the earth be found,
Changed in the twinkling of an eye,
And raised to be with Christ on high;
    This is my hope today.

Forgive each sin and each mistake,
Dear Lord, that I in weakness make;
New faith, and love, and courage give,
That I may to Thy glory live:
    This is my prayer today.

Sunshine and Shadow

Aug. 10, 1939

(Note: one day when it was partly cloudy, my little boy asked me, "Mommy, why does Jesus keep turning the sun on and off?")

Why should there come into my life
First much of sun, then much of strife?
Sometimes the sun shines very bright,
Then shadows come and veil the light;
Often when skies are blue and fair,
Dark clouds arise with pain and care.

I do not know the answer, still
I am resigned to my Lord's will;
If it pleases Him, I only know,
I would not change the atmosphere,
Because my Lord has placed me here.

For what He sends can only be
The very best there is for me;
And when I travel paths of pain,
He is near and that is gain;
Yes, I can trust Him as my Guide-
My part is only to abide.

Why should deep sorrow come a while?
I do not know but I can smile
And say to Him, "Thy will be done,"
Till once again He sends the sun.
And when in heav'n His face I see,
The shadows all will have to flee.

Gary's note: the sun would come for both in the spring next year.

Thy Will Be Done
August 12, 1939

Thy will be done, Lord;
     I will not question Thee,
But if in loneliness of heart,
I sigh or let a teardrop start,
     Be patient, Lord, with me.

Thy will be done, Lord;
     I know it's best this way,
But teach me how to hush the sigh,
To brush the teardrop from my eye,
     On Thee my burden lay.

Thy will be done, Lord;
     I do not ask Thee why,
Just help me rise above the trial,
And through it all display a smile,
     Thy name to glorify.

Gary's note: it has been a year since she entered OSTH. She is apparently still contagious.

My Shepherd
Nov. 9, 1939

THE LORD is my Shepherd:
The Lord who all things created,
The Lord who runs the universe,
The Lord who sent His Son to die
To save me from sin's awful curse,
The Lord who is beginning and end-
This same Lord is more than a Friend.

The Lord IS my Shepherd:
Not in some far-off future day,
But in the present, He is near
To guide and keep my faltering steps,
To cast out every doubt or fear-
This God of strength who's quick to see
And every moment care for me.

The Lord is MY Shepherd:
My very own is this great Lord-
With piercing eye He singles me
From out a boundless multitude;
This by His Word I now can see;
For He is my own Shepherd dear
Who cares so lovingly for me here.

The Lord is my SHEPHERD:
And a good shepherd is one
Who guards and cares well for His sheep;
No evil can harm me, no foe can destroy,

For my Shepherd goes never to sleep;
So I have peace because I am His-
The matchless Lord my Shepherd is.

A Mother's Prayer

May 29, 1940
"I will be a God unto thee, and to thy seed after thee." Genesis 17:7

"To thy seed after thee" - I see a promise here
For the salvation of the children who are dear.

"To thy seed after thee" - I know it will be true,
For Thou hast said, and Thou wilt surely do.

God of my salvation, wilt Thou bring them to see
That Jesus died for them on the accursed tree;
Then keep them true to Thee in both word and deed,
By thy infinite grace supplying every need.

And amid the stress of sorrow, trial, or pain,
Truly a God of comfort prove Thyself again;
A solid rock of refuge be to them revealed,
A very present Help, a strong tower, and a shield.

And I would pray Thee, Lord, that Thou wilt never cease
To be unto each one the wondrous God of peace.
May they all know that perfect peace beyond degree,
Which only comes to those whose minds are stayed on Thee.

This is the thing I ask O blessed Lord divine
Just this one request for each dear child of
mine.
I only pray that Thou to them wilt ever be
The very selfsame God that Thou hast been to
me.

*Gary's note: written after coming home after
two years at OSTH. This is her prayer.*

A Prayer
September 30, 1940

"He took the seven loaves and the fishes,
and broke them, and gave to his disciples,
and the disciples to the multitude." Mark 15:36.

I would take into my hands
The bread which Thou dost break,
And in my turn anew to hearts
This bread of life would take.

I would now receive from Thee
The spirit of sacrifice,
A heart broken by they love,
Willingness to pay the price.

Of Thine own human burden,
The burden of sympathy
For the want and woes of man,
I would receive from Thee.

I would ask of Thee Thy best,
The gift that's most divine;
The power and the will to give
I would that these be mine.

A Little Bit of Prayer
Spring 1940

Just a little season of prayer
At the starting of the day,
And that day is made the brighter,
Because you stopped to pray.

Just a little prayer for wisdom
When your own is at an end,
And your problem soon as solved
God will needed wisdom send.

Just a little minute of prayer
When your heart is touched with grief
Will do wonders to uphold you,
Bring a measure of relief.

Just a little prayer for guidance
When you know not what to do,
And somehow He'll lead you out
In the way He's planned for you.

Just a little moment of prayer
When the end of patience nears,
In a fresh supply He'll give you,
New serenity appears.

Just another season of prayer
At the closing of the day,
And your slumber will be sweeter,
Because you stopped to pray.

His Way

December 10, 1940

"His way is perfect." Ps. 18:30

"His way is perfect" -I read it o'er;
What blest assurance! I need no more.
Though my heart is bruised by blows from His
hand,
Yet the way is perfect that He has planned;
If that way He should with heartache fill,
Still I must trust Him and bow to His will.

If mine is the way of pain and care,
His wisdom alone has placed me there,
So I'll trust His love as I go along,
And when faith grows stronger, He'll send the
song;
I could not choose a perfect way,
But when God leads, I cannot stray.

In trusting the Lord I find relief
From the burden of heartache and grief;
In the midst of trial I can rejoice,
And find peace in knowing He makes the choice.
I can never doubt the Lord's decree-
I know His way is perfect for me.

"He Careth For You"
1 Peter 5:7b

He careth for you—He makes it clear;
He careth for you—you need not fear;
If you think His care is not manifest,
Then trust His way as the way that is best;
He careth for you in countless ways,
And His care should bring forth songs of praise.

He careth for you when tests arise,
And Satan comes in tempting guise
From the narrow path to lead you astray—
Of escape for you God will make a way;
You need never know defeat, for He
Has faithfully promised victory;

He careth for you when life is fair,
Even made smooth by His very care;
He careth for you, so do not forget
It is God who is caring for you yet—
The way will be sweet if you walk along
With the Lord of peace, of mirth, and of song.

He careth for you—He loves you still,
Though life with sorrow and care He fill:
He will give you peace to banish the care;
There is joy in sorrow He helps to bear;
Yet will He keep you close to His side,
Teach you more fully in Him to abide.

He careth for you–O promise secure!
He careth for you–for doubt a cure!
He careth for you–Lord, help _me_ to see;
In seeming darkness or in the sunshine
Make me thankful for this care of Thine.

Songs in the Night

March 7, 1941

"In the night His song shall be with me." Ps. 42:8

"Who giveth songs in the night." Job 35:10

His song of eternal salvation
In the deep night of sin;
His song of precious promise
For doubt or fear within;
His song to buoyant hope
In the night of near despair;
His song of sweet relief
In the night of burdensome care;
His song of forgiveness granted
When failure I must confess;
His song of healing comfort
In the night of sore distress;
His song of a perfect peace
In the dark night of sorrow;
His song of quiet patience
O'er what may be tomorrow;
His song of implicit trust
For every test and trial;
His song of true thanksgiving,
Even when there's denial;
The song of His blessed Word:
"I will never leave thee,"
For the ache of a lonely heart–
All these God gives to me.

Reflection
April 1941

Have I led some to believe, Lord,
Ought that is not true?
If so, I bow my head in shame-
Lord, search me through and through!
O, make me all they think I am,
These friends so loving and true!
Remove all vestige of pretense,
Purity of heart renew.
The graces that they seem to find,
Revealed by words of praise,
Perfect in me by all work of grace-
I plead more of Thy ways.

The Way

"I am the Way, the Truth, and the Life." John 14:6a

"I am the Way out of distress;
I am the Way to happiness;
If courage fails and strength is spent,
I am the Way to true content;
In the midst of storm and test
I am the Way to find sweet rest;
If you meet with sorrow today
And comfort seek, I am the way;
Though cares should throng without surcrease,
I am the Way to perfect peace;
When it is with trouble you meet,
I am the Way of refuge sweet;
If there should to you come grief,
I am the Way to find relief;
If an answer to prayer you seek,
I am the Way through whom to speak;
I am the Way, the Truth, the Life-
I conquer death, and sin, and strife."

Rest

June 6, 1941
"Rest in the Lord." Ps. 37:7

Rest? When storm clouds gather
And darkness fills my days?
Rest? When the cares of life
Choke back the springs of praise?
Rest? When anxious fears
My heart and mind beset?
Rest? When the future holds
Small ray of hope as yet?

Rest? When problems puzzle
And for solution clamor?
Rest? When dreadful doubts
With insistence hammer?
Rest? When my heart is grieved
Over each past mistake?
Rest? When loneliness brings
A dull, persistent ache?

Rest! Yes, I can rest,
Rest in the Lord and be still,
A quietness securing
By bowing to His will,
Casting all care on Him,
Trusting His way is best;
For His promises true
Cause the weary to rest.

In Trouble

Aug. 9, 1941

"God is our Refuge and Strength, a very present
help in trouble." Ps. 46:1

God does not promise deliverance
From the sorrow that wounds the heart,
But only whenever there is grief,
He will comfort and strength impart;
In His Word it is not promised
That all trials soon shall cease,
Only His grace suffices,
To the troubled heart sends peace.

God nowhere gives us assurance
That from trouble we shall be free,
But He Himself is our Refuge,
Our Support and Shelter is He;
He does not agree that problems
Will not perplex nor confound,
But we go to Him for guidance-
There His wisdom and help are found.

He does not always insure
To deliver us from distress,
But he gives succor in the testing,
And the burden and care are less;
A present help in our troubles
Is the Lord, our Refuge and Strength,
And our trials and grief and heartache
Shall be turned into joy at length.

Because I Have Not Prayed
1942

Victory promised, the war news is good;
A sense of security appears;
When suddenly dire changes loom
Again our hearts are heavy with fears-
Because I have not prayed?

Though firmly resolved not to speak the word
That genders strife, nor to seek men's praise,
Just to let God have His way in my life,
I have often failed in many ways-
Because I have not prayed?

Speaking to others of God's salvation
Holding forth Christ as the way, the light,
I have met with scorn or indifference
And refusal to turn to the right-
Because I have not prayed?

Loved ones have drifted away from the Lord,
Farther and farther from Him it seems,
And others ne'er known my Savior,
Or fellowship with the one who redeems-
Because I have not prayed?

Could each of these things have come to pass
When need of more prayer I did not see?
Could my feeble prayers really count so much?
Lord, forgive! Again may it not be
Because I have not prayed.

Questioning
1942

"And why call me Lord, Lord, and do not
The things which I say?" Luke 6:46

"You call Me 'Lord' and obey me not-
What cruel mocking is this?
Is your love pretense, like Judas',
Who betrayed me with a kiss?

"You call Me 'Lord' and "Master,' too,
But am I Lord of your life,
When envy and anger are present,
And pride and malice, and strife?

"You call Me 'Lord' and do not the things
I command you in my Book,
And there are days when you never
E'en within its pages look.

"You call Me 'Lord' and grieve Me,
Break My loving heart anew
By sinful thoughts, or words, or deeds,
When I long to have all of you.

"You call Me 'Lord' and neglect to pray,
To seek of your risen Lord
Power for walk and service, knowing
Victory is the reward.

"Why say to Me 'Lord, Lord,' my child,
And of fresh crucify Me,
By following Me afar off,
When I yearn to be all to thee?"

Let Not Your Heart Be Troubled
1943
John 14:1a

"Let not your heart be troubled
Over those sins of the past-
I am even able to make mistakes
Redound to my glory at last;
Forgetting those things which are behind,
Seek a closer walk with Me to find.

"Let not your heart be troubled,
Though your loved ones wander far
From abundant life in Me,
Or still in darkness are;
I have heard thy prayers and seen thy tears
Our God the cry of His children hears.

"Let not your heart be troubled,
Fraught with anxious care or fear-
I will take your burdens upon Myself,
If you'll only leave them here:
Have not I promised to care for you?
Then what can your needless worry do?

"Let not your heart be troubled:
Leave those sick ones to My care;
I am the Great Physician
Who watches over them there.
I loved them enough for them to die,
So trust that love, nor question why.

"Let not your heart be troubled;
My peace I give unto you,
And nothing can take it away-
My promise is ever true.
So leave all to My loving hand,
Just trust though you do not understand.

Prayer for a Sailor Lad
1943

I do not ask Thee that he always
Shall from all danger be kept free,
But only that when peril nears,
Thy peace his shield and trust shall be;
If he is lonely or downhearted, Lord,
May the memory of his mother's voice, her
prayers
Compel him to seek his mother's God,
To find the solace for loneliness and cares
Often I plead for his safe return
From battle zones, but just now
I pray only for this greater need;
Keep him from evil by Thy grace somehow.
But if his time must come to die,
May his heart calmly and unafraid abide
Because his trust is placed in One,
The Lord Christ Jesus-He who also died.

*(Written during the war for the son of a dear
friend.)*

Thoughts While Ironing
February 2, 1944

Today while ironing, across every piece
Back and forth, up and down the board without
cease
My iron moved, smoothing the wrinkles out;
Then I reflected how God had moved to rout
My sin, covering it with the blood of Christ
when
Taking all of my guilt, Jesus made me whole
again.

As I worked sometimes I missed a corner there
Leaving wrinkles; and I lifted a prayer
To the Father, asking his Spirit to move
To take away that which He might disapprove,
To come into the inmost recesses of my heart
To expose sin to light and bid it depart.

And I thought, as my iron moved in and out
How God smooths each wrinkle of fear, or of
doubt,
Of worry, of heartache, of troublesome care,
Of sorrow, of trial, or of despair,
Leaving only unruffled calm and His cheer,
And more steadfast faith in His promises dear.

If the smooth fabric became wrinkled again,
The iron removed every trace-and then
I though how often it's true in my life

That it is made ugly by sins or strife;
But when full confession I make to the Lord,
He cleanses from sin, and I am restored.

As I dwelt on these truths-old, and yet new-
Before I knew it, my ironing was through!

Gary's note: Written when she arrived home again.

Logic

"If God be for us, who can be against us?"
Romans 8:31a

If God be for me, then I need not fear
Even this conflict I am dreading so;
Before opinions of mere men, though wise,
I need not falter when this fact I know.

If God be for me, and I know He is,
He will uphold me, though I stand alone
To battle all their learned arguments,
Forceful, since their truth I must own.

And yet one thing stands out above the rest:
I must, I will obey my Lord's command;
What matters that the flesh trembles and
shrinks,
If God be for me, true to Him I'll stand.

The cost? It does not matter, since He knows,
And all things for my good are working here;
I will trust Him and, resting, be at peace;
If God is for me, there is naught to fear.

Gary's note: Written concerning the doctor's counsel that she should abort her unborn child in 1946. It did cost her; she ended up in OSTH for a third time. This son would go on to become a pastor for twenty years.

God's Way

1947

"This is <u>the</u> way, walk ye in it." Isaiah 30:21

"Crushed 'neath the burdens you are called to
bear?"
<u>My</u> way is to cast upon me your care?
Disappointed because the path is so rough?
<u>My</u> way is perfect-is not that enough?
Tired in body, in mind distressed?
<u>My</u> way says, "come unto me and rest."
Afraid for the future, hopes in dust laid?
<u>My</u> word instructs thee to "be not afraid",
Under the pressure, fearful of failing me?
<u>My</u> promise, "my grace is sufficient for thee."
Perplexed, questioning the reason why?
That this is <u>my</u> way should satisfy.
Sick with the helplessness of regret?
<u>My</u> way is press onward, the past forget."

Whatever may come, "this is <u>the</u> way,
Walk ye in it," to me Thou dost say;
I stand rebuked, my precious Lord--
Peace and confidence are restored.

*Gary's note: She had to return to OSTH for a
third time after refusing to have an abortion.*

Trusting

August 12, 1947

"Though He slay me, yet I will trust in Him."

I am so glad I have the Lord to trust;
I know His judgements are righteous and just;
Though long and weary are the lonely days,
Blessings remain for which to give Him praise;
Trial and loneliness are with me yet,
Still peace is mine, for He does not forget.

And this my trust is based upon His Word:
In reading there my heart is always stirred;
He has said He will not fail me, nor forsake,
And that He knows the way that I must take;
The comfort that it brings I cannot tell,
When this I read, "He hath done all things
well."

Though He should slay me, I will trust in Him
To keep me through death's shadow dark and
dim;
I will awaken on the other side,
To dwell with Him who here has been Guide;
Though He slay me, I will trust Him to mind-
And do the best for those I leave behind.

Surrender

1949

"Ye are not your own, for ye are bought with a price." 1 Cor. 6:19, 20

If I am not my own,
But Christ has purchased me,
Delivered me at such a price,
His servant I must be.

If I am not my own,
Nothing I have is mine;
Now with myself and family,
I all to him consign.

If I am not my own,
Nothing is left to chance;
He will guard His property
In every circumstance.

A Song in the Wilderness
March 7, 1950
"I will...bring her into the wilderness...and I will
give her vineyards from vineyards from thence..
and she shall sing there." Hosea 2:14

There is a wilderness in my life,
But there is planted a vineyard too;
Dreary and dry is the wilderness,
For suffering is not easy it's true;
Yet God's presence a wonderful vineyard makes
In the midst of a wilderness of heartaches.

A vineyard found in a desert place
Is a thing of beauty to the eyes;
The green leaves in abundance growing
And the luscious fruit we highly prize;
And His face is beautiful even through tears,
Peace insured by His presence, in spite of fears.

Vineyards are planted food to provide,
To sustain and nourish life in man,
But one taste of fruit is never enough,
One must return again and again;
Thus I feast on God's word in time of duress,
His promises nourish my soul in distress.

A satisfying drink can also be made
By pressing juice from fruit of the vine -
It is nectar to the thirsty one,
This purple, bubbling sparkling wine;

My thirsty soul drinks now the fountain of love
My longing heart satisfied by God above.

*Gary's note: her eldest daughter was to
graduate high school the following June.
Florence did, however, get to see her graduate.*

Who Will Go?
November 25, 1950
(After reading the tract, "One Jungle Night.")

There are many marching along life's way
To the edge of a cliff that falls away
To the depths of a Christ-less eternity,
Unless they are warned by you or by me.

Can't you hear the tramp of those marching
feet,
Rushing on to hell with every heartbeat?
Who will go caution the blinded throng
As they near the brink, ere they fall headlong?

Along the edge some sentinels are seen,
But with many unguarded gaps between,
Men plunge in their blindness wholly unwarned,
So their souls are lost, and by God are mourned.

"Who will go for us, and whom shall I send?"
Asks the Lord, "On whom can I quite depend
To warn the lost of their oncoming doom,
Except in their hearts for Me they make
room?"

The Lord needs sentries to guard the rim,
Turn blind men from death and back to Him;
For they're moving onward to surest hell,
Unless there is someone to go and tell.

Giving Thanks

September 3, 1951

"In everything give thanks." 1 Thessalonians
5:18

Through tears giving Thee thanks -
For Thou has said I must;
I thank Thee for this trial
That teaches me to trust;
I even thank thee for the pain
That seems so hard to bear,
For anything is good that brings
The patience found in prayer.

For woe that brings heart-searching
And repentance for neglect,
For lessons learned in sorrow
Thou dost my praise expect;
For things I cannot understand
My thanks to thee I bring -
In spite of aching heart, I will
Give thanks in everything.

Gary's note: Perhaps written about the oldest twin's lung surgery. He finished high school while at OSTH. He would go on to live a fulfilling life until his passing on March 25, 2007.
I marvel as I feel my mother's pain, and wonder at her trust in her Lord and submission to his will. Would I? Would you?

Inclusion
Oct. 8, 1951

Anytime I want an audience
Before the throne of grace
Of heaven's King, my Father,
He's sure to hear my case;
I can have the time to thank Him
For His blessings on the way,
Or present my needs before Him,
Take it minute, hour, or day.

Anywhere I lift my heart up,
The dear Lord hears my prayer;
Whether walking, working, on my knees,
I always find Him there;
At work or play, at home, abroad,
With the Lord I can commune,
And He'll reply as He knows best,
Though He answers late or soon.

Anyone can come to Jesus,
By prayer can seek His face,
Be he rich or poor, weak or strong,
For all there is a place-
For black or white, for yellow, red,
For the young or for the old;
The prerequisite is faith in Him-
Then blessings He will unfold.

The Valley of Service
Feb 21, 1952

When we go with the Lord Jesus
To the mountaintop to pray,
It is there we are His glory,
It is there we long to stay;
Because of the light of His presence
It is good for us to be there,
Alone with Jesus only
In the fellowship of prayer.

Though we would stay on the mountain,
Still that is never his plan-
With the Savior we must go down
To the valley of service again,
Down to the wounded and helpless,
Down to the sick and diseased,
To bring them unto the Savior,
From their sin to be released.

In the valley people are waiting,
Lost and undone they stand,
Waiting there for Jesus' voice,
The healing touch of His hand;
But we are the tools he uses-
The work to us He surrenders;
If we fail Him, He has no other-
We alone are His messengers.

Psalm 27
March 23, 1952

The Lord is my Light and Salvation:
Of whom shall I be afraid?
God is the very strength of my life,
And He will come to my aid;
When my enemies come upon me,
My foes as a host be sent,
Still my heart shall never be fearful
In this I am confident.
I have desired of the Lord
I will seek after one thing:
To see the beauty of the Lord,
Spend my days in His dwelling;
He shall in the time of trouble
In his pavilion hide me,
Set me upon a rock above
My enemies beside me;
Therefore I will joyfully
Unto the Lord sing praise.
Have mercy upon me, Lord,
Hear when my voice I raise;
Thou said, "Seek ye my face,"
And when I heard Thee speak,
My heart said unto Thee,
"Thy face, Lord, will I seek."
Hide not Thy face from me;
Put not Thy servant away;
Leave me not, neither forsake;
Thou hast ever been my stay;

Though my father and mother forsake me
The Lord will still remain.
Teach me to follow in Thy way,
Lead in a path that's plain.
Deliver me not to my enemies;
False witnesses rise against me.
I had fainted unless I had belived
Yet the goodness of God to see.
Be thou of good courage;

-ending cut off-

Isaiah 53
March 17, 1952

Who hath believed our report?
To whom is God's arm revealed?
He shall grow as a root from dry ground,
A tender plant of the field;
He hath no comeliness nor beauty
That we should desire Him whom we see.
He is despised and rejected of men,
A man acquainted with grief;

He has carried our griefs and sorrows
That He might bring us relief;
He was smitten of God, and afflicted,
Wounded for our sins was he;
He was bruised for our iniquities,
Healed with His stripes are we.
All we like sheep have gone astray,
Have turned each one to his own way,
But all of the world's iniquity
The Lord on Him hath laid.
He is brought as a lamb to slaughter,
And yet no answer made;
He was taken from prison and judgement
(His generation who shall declare?)
Was cut off from the land of the living;
He the sins of my people did bear.
He made His grave with the wicked,
Buried with the rich was He,
Though He had done no violence,

Nor spoken deceitfully.
Yet is pleased the Lord to bruise Him:
His suffering of soul has satisfied.
When Thou madest Him an offering;
By His knowledge many He justified.
I will give Him a portion with the great,
And He shall divide with the strong,
Because He hath poured out His soul to death,
Was numbered with those who did wrong;
For many He bore the transgression,
And for sinners made intercession.

Psalm 1
March 22, 1952

Blessed is the man that walketh not
In the counsel of the ungodly,
Nor stands in the way of sinners
Nor with scornful men sittith he;
In the law of the Lord is his delight-
In it doth he meditate day and night.
And he shall be like a tree
Whose leaf shall never die,
Planted by streams of water;
His fruit shall multiply;
And whatsoever he findeth to do
It shall always prosper there unto.
But the ungoldly are like the chaff
Which the wind driveth away;
They cannot stand in the judgement,
Neither with the righteous stay;
The way of the righteous the Lord will cherish,
But the way of the ungodly shall perish

Love

1 Corinthians 16:14 and 1 Corinthians 13:4-8

Love never fails for it is kind;
With it no evil comes to mind;
It bears all things and suffers long,
Enduring every sort of wrong;
Love's nature harbors not envy,
Or behaves itself unseemly,
Never rejoices in iniquity,
But always in truth and charity;
It's own good it does not seek,
Never is puffed up, but meek,
Does not flaunt itself nor boast,
To quick anger is not host.
Lord of faith, hope, love-these three-
Give of this greatest gift to me!

March 27, 1952
Psalm 19

The heavens declare God's glory;
The firmament showeth His reach;
Night unto night showeth knowledge,
And each day utterth speech;
There is no speech nor language
Where their voices cannot be heard;
Their line is gone out through earth
To the end of the world their word.
In the heavens the Lord hath set
A tabernacle for the sun, which is as a
bridegroom coming,
Or a man as a race to run;
He goeth forth in the heavens,
His circuit he doth repeat
In space from end to end each day;
There is naught hid from his heat.
The Law of the Lord is perfect,
Converting the soul of man;
All the statutes of God are right,
Rejoicing the heart again;
God's testimony is sure,
Making the simple wise;
The Lord's commandment is pure,
Enlightening the eyes;
The fear of the Lord is clear,
Enduring on forever;
The judgements of God are true,
And righteous altogether,

More to be desired than gold,
Sweeter to the taste than honey;
By them thy servant is warned,
In keeping rewarded is he.
Who can understand his errors?
From secret faults cleanse me,
Make innocent of transgression,
From presumptuous sins keep free.
Let my meditations of heart
And the words of my mouth be,

Untitled
April 25, 1952

Wrap your troubles in faith
And give them to God each day,
Tie them with cords of prayer,
And see them vanish away.
Have faith that God loves you,
Believe His purpose is right;
Wrap your troubles in faith,
He will give songs in the night.

Wrap your trials in a promise,
Seal with, "Thy will be done,"
Tie with the ribbons of God's love
To brighten every one.
Trust God's word in darkness-
It shines a lamp for your feet;
Wrap your trials in a promise,
Rest there in peace complete.

To Do Thy Will   May 25, 1952.

"Lo, I come to do Thy will." Hebrews 10:9.

I come to Thee with empty hands;
Nothing within my life I bring,
My heart aglow with one desire:
To give myself as offering.

Prepare me as Thou thinkest best;
When the way is smooth for my feet,
Or roughness causes pain and hurt,
I'll walk by faith in service sweet.

To do Thy will is all I want,
My debt of love remembering, ~~Thy Spirit leading each moment~~
Thy Spirit leading each moment,
Thou the center of all my living.

To Do Thy Will

May 25, 1952

"Lo, I come to do Thy will." Hebrews 10:9

I come to Thee with empty hands;
Nothing within my life I bring,
My heart aglow with one desire;
To give myself as offering.

Prepare me as Thou thinkest best;
When the way is smooth for my feet,
Or roughness causes pain and hurt,
I'll walk by faith in service sweet.

To do Thy will is all I want,
My debt of love remembering.
Thy Spirit leading each moment,
Thou the center of all my living.

Our Blessed Hope
1954

Why should I dread the coming hours,
And with them this new sorrow?
God says He'll give me strength for the day,
And to "take no thought for tomorrow."
This truth comes quickly to mind again;
Jesus may even come before then!

There are days of lonliness ahead,
Days of heartache and of care;
Were it not for the Lord's strong arm,
I would sink into despair;
But all of my ways are to Him known,
And soon He may come back for His own.

Should I worry over tomorrow,
When he gives me peace today?
With the knowledge He ever loves and cares,
And all burdens on Him I lay;
He comforts, and fills my heart with song-
And I'm looking for Him to come ere long.

Bitter Made Sweet
May 5, 1959
"To the hungry soul every bitter thing is sweet."
Proverbs 27:7

Sweet, Lord? When I have met with failure and
defeat,
Your loving heart have wounded-how can that
be sweet?
Yet now your love is sweeter, your forgiveness
dear,
The longing to follow you ever closely here
Is intensified; though it was a bitter thing,
Feeling more my weakness, to you it's sweet to
cling.

Every bitter thing, Lord? This look into my
heart
You give me? What I find pierces like a dart.
Even I abhorrence feel at this revealed sin!
Yet do you, the Holy One, make your home
therein
To fulfill the promise sweet by your words now
willed:
That those who hunger for righteousness shall
be filled.

A bitter cup indeed, this thing I am denied -
How will I without it ever be satisfied?
Even as it arrives, the thought I quickly ban,

You bring me sweet assurance from your word
again:
"God shall supply all your need" lest I should
forget
In constant fellowship with you all needs are
met.

What of disappointment, what of this greater
test
Falling on my heart, that hungers for thy best?
A bitter thing is trial, yet it, too, can be
Made sweet by the knowledge this is your plan
for me.
To the hungry soul who yearns to walk in thy
way,
Each bitter thing is sweetened by thy grace each
day.

Anticipation
December 18, 1959

I wake in the night time, startled
By some sound - - I know not what - -
But sorely disappointed,
I sink back onto my cot;
I thought it was the trump of God,
But no! He cometh not.

I hear a strange and sudden noise,
As my work I go about-
Perhaps it is Jesus coming
From this world to take us out!
Is this the archangel's voice
Or the echo of Christ's shout?

I observe unrest of nations;
With fear men's hearts do quake;
I read of erupting volcanoes,
Of flood and of earthquake;
And I know that soon I will see Him
Who died just for my sake.

As I mingle here with others,
I must speak of Christ to some,
For to those who do not know Him
He'll return as unwelcome;
One shall be taken, the other left,
When the Son of man shall come.

I am to watch for his coming –
These words from His lips are clear;
But in a time of forgetting
(I am so busy down here!)
In an hour when I think not
Then my Savior may appear.

"He is coming, yes, He is coming."
This the theme of my heart's tune;
Perhaps it will be at midnight,
Or again it may be at noon;
All my soul thrills with the knowledge:
Jesus Christ is coming soon.

God's Love

Jan. 16, 1959

Romans 8:35-39

What can separate me from God?
No joy nor sorrow can divide,
Not pain nor peril, life nor death,
Not even my own selfish pride
Can ever change His love for me-
It's deeper than the depths of sin,
Higher than the lofty height
Of any honor I might win.

What can separate me from God?
These every day realities
Have no effect upon His love,
Nor powers nor principalities;
No matter what may be ahead,
E'ery persecution, by word or sword,
Neither distress nor unhappiness
Can alter this love of the Lord.

What can separate me from God?
No devil loosed upon the earth,
No angel watching from on high,
No trial, nakedness, nor death,
No fellow man-not even I,
By disobeying His commands
Can weary such a Love divine,
Nor take myself out of His hands.

Remedy for Defeat
January 20, 1959

"And Jesus...said, Arise, and be not afraid."
Mt. 17:7

The devil strewed rocks on my path one day:
How quickly I stumbled and fell on the way;
But the Lord helped me up, and then once more
I walked on carelessly, as before;
But Satan I found far wiser than I-
Again, never watching, I fell with a sigh;
I was longer arising but I thought
That this was the last time I should be caught.

Limping a little from falling so much,
Trying to keep with my Savior in touch,
I went on more warily than before,
But still I tripped, and grieved Him more;
Then He lifted me up to try a new road,
Yet I was borne down by temptation's load;
Weakly I rose, but I should not remain,
Till I concluded it was all in vain.

Crippled and lame, I lay still at His feet,
Crushed and despairing, admitting defeat.
"Lord, You have failed me!" in anguish I cried,
"For I tried hard to walk close by your side."
"But I want to live in you," He replied,
But you are filled with rebellion and pride."
"I can't live without You!" I said, "Take these,

And whatever else in my life does not please."

He smiled, and gently He bade me arise-
I was afraid, and I answered, with sighs,
"I have not the strength to go on again,
I have no assurance that I can."
"The devil was routed at Calvary,
There your sin-filled self crucified, with Me."
Then I rose, unafraid, to make Him my All-
Because He lives in me, I need not fall.

Christt Within
February 3, 1959
"Looking unto Jesus..." Heb. 12:2a

I look unto Jesus as my Advocate each day
To plead my cause whene'er I sin, stray from
Him away;
To the Father He presents His pierced hands
and feet,
Reminding that by His blood salvation is
complete;
Since my Savior speaks for me, if I confess, God
can
Cleanse from sin and restore to fellowship
again.

I look unto Jesus as once crucified for me:
He paid the penalty for sin that I might be free,
Free not only from sin's guilt, but also from its
power.
Believing that my sinful self died with Him that
hour,
Daily die unto my selfish nature within,
Knowing He has freed me from the dominion of
sin.

I look unto Jesus as not only being near,
As close beside me ever, walking with me here,
But I look unto Him as the One who dwells
within,

Christ in me, the Power of God, able to conquer my sin;
As I look unto Jesus to take complete control,
His righteousness then fills heart and mind and soul.

Tears
Sept. 24, 1959

There are no tears in heaven
I've often heard it said,
But those who make this statement
Have not _my_ Bible read.

There it says that God shall wipe
Away all tears from eyes—
If tears flow not in heaven,
Will it be on this wise?

I think there will be tears up there—
At least, there will be mine,
If those I've shed at failing Him
Down here is any sign.

Will there be tears in heaven?
For a short while there may,
But lovingly, with tender touch,
He'll wipe them all away.

Not For Reward
Oct. 9, 1959

I want God's will in my daily life;
I want each moment to go His way;
I want Him to take complete control
Of each thought and act, the words I say.

But I do not serve my God for gain;
I do not covet crown or reward
That to the faithful He will give-
I do it because I <u>love</u> the Lord.

What care I for a crown in heaven
(Except to cast at my Savior's feet?)
Just seeing my Lord, hearing His voice
Will make My blessing fully complete.

In heaven I only want Jesus
And to be evermore without sin;
Only for love I serve Him down here,
Not for hope of a crown I might win.

"Look Unto Me"
November 12, 1959
Isaiah 45:22

I cannot look at Jesus and not see my own sin,
His holiness reveals I am defiled within;
I cannot look to Jesus and any sin forget;
He'll not let me see His light and live in
darkness yet.

I cannot look at God and live as I did before-
That look permits no tolerance of sin anymore;
I cannot look at Him and stay in my self-
deceit-
The veil is torn from my eyes when I the Savior
meet.

I cannot look at God and live with the least
malice,
Nor can my heart ever grow indifferent and
callous;
I cannot see His love for me shown at Calvary,
And refuse Him anything that He should ask of
me.

One true, revealing look at God always melts
my heart;
And I cannot outside His will remain for long
apart;
His Spirit causes me to look at His love and
grace;
I am forever changed by one look into His face.

Present Salvation

Dec. 6, 1959

"...He shall save His people from their sins." Mt.
1:21

Jesus is not really your Savior
Unless in your life each day
He delivers you from secret faults,
And answers you when you pray;
He cannot be your Savior now,
If you do not let Him live,
His life in you, by yielding,
His own power to you give.
But He is truly your Savior,
And He fully satisfies,
When this power for daily living
For yourself you recognize.

Where Else?

Feb. 26, 1960

"Lord, to whom shall we go?" John 6:68

After each setback, in every fear,
When discouraging trials appear,
In each success or failure in life,
When it all seems just struggle and strife,
Whenever my hopes joyfully shine,
Or thrilling attainment been mine,
If I have a sense of terrible need,
Quickly to Christ I go with all speed.

After each sin that has grieved His heart,
If in souls won I have had a part,
If disappointment sore distresses,
And discouragement on me presses,
When I am filled with joy as I go,
Or all feeling departs, still I know
The Lord is yet near, I trust His grace,
Ever to Him I must turn my face.

When some temptation I can resist,
When some coveted mark I have missed,
After each victory or defeat,
In every new test that I must meet,
After achievement bringing joy,
Or whenever frustrations annoy,
Where can I go in gain or loss
Except to my Savoir of the cross?

He Restores

August 30, 1960

"I will restore you to the years that the locust hath eaten." Joel 2:25

Thou saist, "I will restore" -how, Lord?
My heart is near despair-
Those useless, empty years are gone,
Small fruit borne for Thee there.
But Thou hast said it-blessed word!
I will do what I can
To glorify Thy name henceforth-
O use me once again!

Help me never to grow weary,
In courage never lack,
Nor lose heart over fruitless days
And never to look back;
Time wasted never will return-
Today give me, I ask,
New ways of serving Thee once more,
Some simple, lowly task.

I do not care to have men's praise,
Nor do great things for Thee-
Just keep me mindful every hour
A blessing here to be.
I can't go back and do the things
I should have done before,
But find for me some service now,
Another open door.

Gary's note: Little did our mother know her main ministry would be to the twenty-first century.

Grace
November 15, 1963

Down through eternity God looked,
And singled out my name
As one who should belong to Him,
Then for this purpose came,
Himself to die to ransom me;
Then stormed my heart until,
No longer able to withstand,
I bowed unto His will.

How great my sin would be He saw
(But God is greater still!),
The base rebellion and the pride
That would my being fill;
But grace - His grace - went flowing out
To cleanse my humbled soul -
His no surprise to find the sin
That permeates the whole.

I am His, for He chose me,
Set His love upon me,
Purchased, yes, by Jesus' blood,
Redemption full and free;
May this same grace which operates
Down to my present way
Create desire to will and do
His pleasure day by day.

*Gary's Note: As near as we can tell this was the
year after our father divorced her after 31 years
of marriage.*

Untitled

Fall 1963

The saddest time for the human heart
Is not from its trial and care,
For these can always be taken
To the heavenly Father in prayer;
There He gives courage and comfort;
There is found strength for each day;
There, too, the burden is lifted,
And His Word lights up the way.

And the saddest time for the Christian
Is not when his loved ones depart
To be with the Lord up in heaven,
Though loneliness tears at the heart;
For grief is assuaged by His presence,
The Comforter comes with His cheer
To uphold the one who is mourning,
Reminding of promises dear.

No, the saddest time for a Christian
Is when he has failed the Lord
In some time of severe testing,
And Satan seems to have scored;
For defeat is a bitter experience,
The broken heart reels in dismay
At the grief he has caused his Savior,
And dishonor brought to His way.

It is well to pray for the fallen

Whose life has known these stains;
Though God in His mercy has pardoned,
Discouragement still remains;
There is ache of heart for the knowledge
That his testimony is gone,
And he needs your prayers for the grace
And courage just to go on.

Yes, this is the sorrow of sorrows
To the Christian who loves the Lord,
Though a merciful God has forgiven
And fellowship is restored:
So it's well to pray for another
At these times when faith is low,
Yet much better to ask beforehand
He find strength to vanquish the foe.

Gary's note: Probably written after the divorce.

Neglect
October 30, 1967

Have you ever won a soul to Christ?
If so, how long ago?
Has it been a week, a month a year
Since God used you to show
The Way of the Cross to a weary heart,
Weighted down with his sin,
Since you felt the glorious thrill that comes
As someone enters in?

Perhaps you recall it was your word
That led some soul to Him
Months or years ago, but now
The memory's growing dim;
But what of the days or weeks since then,
What of this very day?
Have you held forth the Word of Life
To a lost soul today?

Has your love for God grown colder
With every passing week,
Your ardor cooled till you seldom dare
Of your Savior dear to speak?
Do you often a heavy-burdened heart
Lift to the Lord in prayer
For those outside the heavenly fold,
Plead their salvation there?

O lord, convict each child of Thine

Who does not heed Thy Word
To spread the gospel everywhere
To those who have not heard,
Convict of sin...for such it is...
And give new love for Thee
And for lost souls, that we may heed
Thy words to us, "Go ye!"

Admonition

"Speak no evil one of another." James 4:11

Speak no evil one of another
This is ever the Christian way,
Yet alas! our hearts condemn us
For the things we often say.

Speak not evil one of another:
Cast the beams from your own eyes
Ere you utter condemnation.
Or another criticize.

You may not know the problems
That beset a Christian brother;
Try overlooking his faults;
Speak not evil one of another.

Speak not evil one of another,
But for one another pray,
And more good will be accomplished
Than in any other way

Afterward

There was stillness after Jesus' death,
A silence in that cave,
Peacefulness after the agony,
Quiet rest in the grave:
After crisis in the human heart,
When self with Him has died,
After the struggle, after the pain,
There comes peace to abide.

That stillness is only found in death,
Death to self and sin,
Quietness and confidence in the Lord,
A waiting deep within.
But Jesus came forth to life again,
Life altogether new,
And one who follows Him in death
Will share in His life, too.

A Gift

"-They-whom Thou hast given Me (Your gift to Me'-A.W.T.)" John 17:24

Lord, I am not a handsome gift
I have been marred by sin,
But you who have accepted me
Can make me clean within;
You can take this sinful heart,
Transform it by your power,
Out of the gift that's given you
Make righteousness to flower.

This gift God gave to you-myself-
Does not amount to much,
But I would give you pleasure
By submitting to your touch;
I want you to manipulate
My every word and deed;
Find me some little service now
To do, just as you lead.

Take now my life into your hands
And mold like to yourself;
Make me into a useful gift,
Not one upon a shelf,
By you set forth that others
Can see that I am thine.
But I want to be a gift for use,
Not just a nice design.

A God at Hand

"Am I a God at hand, saith the Lord, And not a
God afar off?" Jer. 23:23

He is not a God afar off,
But a God who's close at hand;
I cannot hide from Him;
He knows the things I have planned
Before I can carry them out;
He perceives each secret thought;
He knows each trial and and heartache
With which my pathway is fraught.

The Lord is at hand to comfort
In each sorrow, great or small;
If I am perplexed, He's so near
That I have only to call;
To know He will never leave me
Is balm to my lonely heart;
And whenever temptations harass,
He's here His strength to impart.

This precious sense of His nearness
Brings to me such sweet release
From all care, and worry, and fretting,
Leaving only joy and peace;
He says, "I am with you always,"
And I know His searching eye
Rests on me, and I live more uprightly,
Because I know He is nigh.

All Lack is God

Do you have restlessness, a lack of peace
within?
Do you know that uneasiness is produced by sin?
For your iniquities have come between you and
the Lord,
And only can the rest you seek be by Him
restored,
For this lack is God.

Do in life most of your goals you manage to
obtain,
Is there still an emptiness you cannot well
explain?
Is there yet a longing, an unidentified need?
It is the spirit who is come with your soul to
plead,
For that lack is God.

Do your responsibilities tax beyond endurance?
Are there too many burdens that must be borne
at once?
Are you oppressed with a sense of failure or
defeat?
Are you seeking a source of strength these
pressures to meet?
Your lack is God.

Are there serious problems that await decision?

Do your own selfish desires sometimes blur
your vision?
Is it wisdom you are needing to decide alright?
In Jesus Christ alone is found true wisdom and
light;
The lack is God.

Is it difficult to obtain lives necessities?
Are you dissatisfied because others live in ease?
Inexplicable longings, feelings of discontent,
Any need whatever, of small or great extent,
ALL lack is God.

An Hour of Worship

That privilege was mine
To be in God's house today,
To worship and to sing His praise
After some time away,
And to join with others there
In the fellowship hour of prayer.

My heart was filled with joy
As we raised our voices in song,
And the rapture of those moments
Has been with me all day long;
The hymns we there were singing
Still within my heart are ringing.

There as we bowed our heads
And lifted heart and voice
In prayer to our Redeemer,
Then again did I rejoice,
I felt the very essence
Of the Spirit's divine presence.

As I listened to the pastor
Give the message of the morn,
New resolve to serve God better
There within my heart was born;
So deeply was my spirit stirred,
Well I knew it was God's Word.

Something in the fellowship

During such a sacred hour
Draws me closer to my Savior,
Makes me conscious of His power:
And blessings I have gone to seek
Stay with me throughout the week.

Another Way

"They saw the young child...and...they departed
into their own country <u>another way</u>. "
Matthew 2:11, 12

To worship Christ the holy child
The wisemen came to him that day,
But after they had seen his face,
They traveled home another way;
And one who finds Jesus today
Will then walk on another way,
The old familiar paths will leave,
A pattern new of life will weave.

The Child of Bethlehem became
The Savior you can make your own,
Then day by day your life be lived
Another way than you have known.
Will <u>you</u> be a "wise man" today,
Living in a different way,
Or after this Christmas time is o'er,
Will you be the same as before?

A Robin's Song

I heard a robin singing in the rain...
Somehow my heart was cheered by his refrain,
Because he kept that song of joyfulness,
I quickly reasoned I could do no less.

If he could still rejoice amidst the storm,
Just trusting God to keep him safe and warm
Then in the midst of any earthly trial
Surely I can trust Him with a smile.

If in the heart of that small feathered bird
Was born the charming melody I heard,
Although the wind was blowing strong and free
Then I can sing whatever comes to me.

If he could trust his Maker in the rain,
And from that trust a song of gladness gain
Then I have learned a lesson, thanks to him:
I'll trust my Lord even in shadows dim.

In rain and wind and storm that robin sang,
And through my very inmost soul there rang
Resolve to trust my God through good or ill,
To gain a song by loving the Lord's will.

A Song

God gives me a song in the morning,
As the light of the new day breaks;
In the rosy glow of the dawning
Thanksgiving a melody makes;
He gives me a song in the morning
And throughout all the day long,
When around is gladness and light,
His goodness to me is the song.

God gives me a song in the night time,
When darkness falls over the land;
He reveals that this is the right time
To trust in the way He has planned;
He gives me a song in the night time,
When everything seems all wrong;
When the path ahead is darkened,
His presence then is the song.

Beatitudes in Rhyme
Matthew 5:3-12

"Blessed are the poor in spirit,
For they shall heaven gain;
Blessed are they that mourn -
Comfort they shall obtain;
Blessed indeed are the meek,
For they shall inherit the earth;
Blessed those who realize
Of God's righteousness the worth,
Who hunger and thirst after it,
For they shall all be filled;
And blessed are the merciful -
Mercy to them is willed;
Blessed are the poor in heart,
For God's face they shall see;
Blessed are the peacemakers -
Called God's sons they'll be;
Blessed are you when persecuted
All for righteousness' sake -
Thus lived the prophets before you;
All kind of suffering take
Reviling or else accusation -
If you bear it just for me,
Rejoice and be exceedingly glad:
For great your reward shall be."

Be Something for God
"That we should be to the praise of His glory."
Ephesians 1:12a

I must be to the praise of His glory,
Not do, nor work, nor give;
Even witnessing cannot be
As important as how I live.

I must be to the praise of His glory,
Yielding to His control;
Being something for Jesus,
Not doing, is my goal.

I must be to the praise of His glory...
Giving of time or means
Indication is of His Spirit
Working behind the scenes.

I must be to the praise of His glory...
Holiness is God's doing;
For His Spirit alone gives the power,
These other things ensuing.

"Carest Thou Not?"
Mark 4:38

Carest Thou not there's an ache in my heart,
That these burdens I bear make teardrops
start?
Carest thou not that sore trials oppress?
Carest thou not for my deep distress?
Carest thou not for my sorrow and pain,
Or do I cry unto Thee all in vain?
Carest thou not for my soul's bitter grief?

Chosen

"I have chosen <u>you</u>." John 15:16

"I have chosen <u>you</u>," He said.
Lord, how could you have chosen me,
When you could see I'd fail you so,
In my own way walk willfully?
"I knew all this when I chose you . . .
Your sin I never can condone,
But I died there on Calvary
That for <u>this</u> sin I might atone."

But, Lord, my heart is near despair,
Nowhere I look is there a light;
I brought dishonor to Your name
By counting not upon Your might;
And to sin for a little while,
Self-deceived, I yielded still,
My wicked heart my own downfall,
Because I did not <u>want</u> Your will.

"Yes, My child, you have done well
Humbly to own the fault all yours,
For only this forgiveness brings,
Once more My cleansing full secures.
Do not despair My child, for I
The end from the beginning knew;
Pause now but to remember
That <u>knowing this</u>, <u>Yet I chose you</u>.

"Chastisement always follows sin:

A man must reap whate'er he sows,
But when the broken, contrite heart
A true repentance to Me shows,
"All things-e'en this-do work for good."
I now this promise to you give:
New blessing and service await that one
Who for My glory now will live."

Christmas Away From Home

Seldom is there it ever found
A time of loneliness so deep
As that which penetrates the heart
When Christmas season one must keep
Alone, or with strangers about,
Away from the friends and family;
Though eyes refuse to shed a tear,
The bravest heart weeps silently.

And yet there is the unique sense
Of oneness with the Christ who came
From heaven, here to dwell with men
He must have felt somewhat the same;
He must have missed his fathers home,
The worship that the angels gave
Much more than we can realize,
When he came down our souls to save.

But Christmas is a blessed time,
No matter where we are on the earth,
For ones who know the true purpose
Of the Lord Jesus' lowly birth,
For Jesus cheers all the loneliness,
And he knows all of the sorrow,
And the carols we sing of his birth
Speak hope, of his coming tomorrow.

Christmas Preparations

With joy we wrap our Christmas gifts,
And on each card we write
The names of friends and family
With satisfaction bright;
<u>With sorrow</u> God sent forth His Son
From His home in heaven;
Labelled "for a lost, dying world,"
Jesus Christ was given.

Our hearts aglow with happiness,
Our presents we prepare,
But God's heart ached to see His Son
Wrapped in the form of a babe
And made of low estate
Here to become vile sin for us -
Ne'er was a gift so great!

Let us receive this Gift of gifts
Into our lives to stay,
With cleansed hearts prepare Him room,
Not just on Christmas day,
But every day throughout the year
Be temples fully clean
And meet for Him to dwell within,
Now that His love is seen.

Christmas

To many Christmas is a time
Of fun, frivolity, and, too,
A merry round of gay parties,
Of dancing, playing whole nights through:
A time to decorate, you know,
With holly wreaths and mistletoe,
Place gifts for friends and family
Beneath a festive Christmas tree –
Forgetting why it should be so.

But here's what Christmas means to me:
Truly a time to celebrate,
The happiest day of all the year,
The day when we commemorate
The birth of Jesus long ago
Into our world here below,
God's greatest gift to man, and we,
With grateful hearts, in memory,
Our gifts on others bestow.

Consolation

"And the inhabitant shall not say, I am sick."
Isaiah 33:24.

Rejoice, ye save of the Lord!
We shall say "I am sick " no more
When break eternity's morning
Over on that other shore.
What comfort to those in illness,
What a Solace to those in pain
To know that in God's tomorrow
Will Never be sickness again!

Welcome words to those who are weary
With suffering and long for rest
Their heads will there be pillowed
Safely on the savior's breast;
Words of hope for those who languish
On beds of sickness for a space-
The Lord has provided in heaven
An eternal resting-place.

Those who sorrow here in affliction
In heaven God will repay;
Over there in the glory-land
Their sighing shall flee away;
The eyes that are blinded on earth
It His beauty the king shall see -
Those eyes will no more dim
In the land of eternity.

The ears of the deaf shall be opened;
The tongue of the dumb shall sing
Songs of everlasting praise
To the Healer and their King;
The stammerers shall speak plainly,
As a hart the lame man leaps,
For they all shall be made whole,
Every joy and gladness reap.

Rejoice that the Lord has written
In the book of life your name!
In the shade of the tree of life
We shall nevermore exclaim
Over suffering, nor sadly say,
"I am sick", but shall have rest
Beneath it's healing leaves,
Evermore in heaven blessed.

Content

I am content, though this distressing trial
Deprives me of so much I count worthwhile;
Sometimes my heart aches for the joy and bliss
Of days gone by with loved ones I now miss,
Yet I'm content because my Lord is near -
He takes my hand and travels with me here.

I am content, for if my heart should fail
For fear of what the future may unveil,
He knows what is waiting each coming day,
He knows and He has planned for me my way;
I trusting when I cannot understand,
I will leave each tomorrow in His hand.

I am content: When I look back and see
The sins that sent Him to the cross for me,
I see the greatness of His love divine
And that His care and blessing all are mine;
His love for me has passed the supreme test -
I am content in that great love to rest.

Contrast

How do I know you live in the darkness?
Because I have found the light.
How do I know you are spiritually blind?
Because I have been given sight.
How do I know you are lost, as well?
Because God saved me, so I can tell.

I realized not I was in the dark,
Until Jesus Christ drew near,
And the light of His glorious gospel
Made the darkness disappear.
Now I long to lead you to the Light,
For you are still lost in the night.

I never knew I walked blindly,
Until with understanding
I saw Him who was crucified for me
As my Savior, Lord, and King.
O that you realized your true plight,
Would let Jesus come to give you sight:

I knew not what it meant to be lost
Till Christ came to dwell within,
Then I learned He had saved me from death
And the consequences of sin..
He's waiting to do the same for you,
If you will offer Him your heart, too.

Dawning

The joy and peace had fled out of my heart;
Sin shut out all but distant rays of light;
I took my eyes off the Son of righteousness,
And all about me settle down the night.
I saw naught but the pain and tears,
The trials that so often came my way;
My heart was bitter o'er disappointments
And the cares that's sorely beset each day.

Then slowly, as the dawn breaks in the east,
I saw the hardness of my sinful heart,
The base ingratitude, with barreness of soul-
I cried out for the light God could impart.
I realized then the greatness of His love,
Although ungrateful I had been for long;
Confession then brought back again my peace,
And once more in my heart was born a song.

That song is one of thankfulness to Him
For blessings that I could not see before:
His word, His presence, and His tender care;
And of the temporal things abundant store;
Friendships and love, and laughter on my way;
The trees and sky and flowers that I love.
All of my cares seem insignificant
In the day of fellowship with my God above.

Divine Comfort
December 31, 1938

"He healeth the broken in heart, and blindeth
up their wounds." Psalms 147:3

Though the world is filled with sorrow,
"He health the broken in heart,"
Lifts the curtain drawn over each woe,
Bid doing the night depart.
How real the compassionate Christ
When cometh grief or disease;
Only the hand of a loving God
Can bind such wounds as these.

Bitterness attendant with sorrow
Melts at the touch of His hand,
At the depth of tenderness in His voice,
"Your pathway I have planned."
All the deep, unending heartbreak
God can soothe, and lovely He,
For there flow from His heart of love
Rich streams of sympathy.

Midst the gloom of disappointed hopes,
The despair of an aching heart,
His gracious design may be to teach
The comfort He can impart;
Human sympathy cannot reach
To the depths of a woe untold,
But our hearts adoringly echo
Those words of the psalmist of old.

Easter Tidings

"And go quickly and tell - - - that He is risen
from the dead." Matthew 28:7

Go quickly and tell though He was slain
For your sin and mine, yet He lives again;
When you speak of the mocking, the cross, the
grave,
Add that these only have no power to save - - -
Tell quickly no longer He remains with the
dead,
He now lives to make intercession instead.

Go quickly and tell how He lives every day
To lighten the sorrow we meet on life's way,
To soften the pain and to take away care - - -
In each of our burdens this Jesus is there.
How can the glad hearts of all of His own
Rejoice that He lives and not make it known?

Go quickly and tell He is risen to give
Victory over sin and the power to live
A life more abundant , reflecting His glory:
Go quickly, go quickly and tell the blest story:
How he saves our souls by the death that He
chose,
And is able to keep because He arose.

Exchange

I gave to the Lord Jesus - - what?
Only the thing that sent
My Savior to the cruel cross,
And willingly He went.

I gave to the Lord Jesus - what?
The sin that brought His death,
The suffering that broke His heart
With His last dying breath.

He gave to me for this - what?
Only the thing that meant
Salvation, and I travel on
Rejoicing, heaven sent.

The Lord Jesus gave me - - what?
Life from His wounded hand -
Why the exchange is so unfair
I cannot understand.

Faith vs. Feeling

They say I'm still sick
(Though I do not feel so)
That I must rest longer
Before I'm able to go
Back home to my work,
My duties of old–
This is the opinion
That the doctors hold.

Because doctors know
About physical need,
Even though I feel well,
Their advice I will heed;
Just so, I believe
What God does reveal;
I trust in His Word,
And not how I feel.

If it does not seem so
Because I feel "blue,"
That He's here beside me,
Is it any less true?
He says, "From sin's power
You now shall be free"
It's faith and not feeling
That gives victory.

Sometimes when I've lost
All the joy from my heart,

There immediately comes
The devil's swift dart:
"The blessings you've lost!"
"Not so," I reply,
"For I must on the Lord,
Not on feeling, rely."

Even when I am sad,
For the moment distressed,
I have learned not on moods
Or on feelings to rest;
The feeling may change,
The mood may depart,
But nothing can take
God's peace from my heart!

Fill Me

Fill me with Thy Sprit, Lord,
Fill me till I overflow
With Thy love and with Thy joy,
And I forth to others go
With the story of Thy grace,
Thy salvation full and free;
Fill me so those others may
By Thy power be drawn to Thee.

Fill me with a mighty fullness,
That I bear much fruit for Thee;
I would follow in the footsteps
Of the Man of Galilee,
With a great magnetic power
Unto Him all men He drew:
Fill me with this self-same Spirit
Who will draw men to Him, too.

As I abide and trust in Him,
I would walk e'er as He walked;
With a Spirit-Controlled tongue,
I would talk e'en as He talked,
Seeking only to glorify Him
Who freely gave His all for me-
Fill me with Thy Spirit, Lord,
That my desire may granted be.

Flowers

As I look on the beautiful flowers of God,
What do those flowers mean to me?
Each lovely one has a lesson to teach-
These things in some of the flowers, I see:

First to catch my eye is the crimson rose-
I think of my scarlet sins, of the flow
Of Christ's precious blood on Calvary's cross
That has washed them whiter than snow.

It stands for the royalty of my King,
This purple pansy which next I see-
The divine glory of a matchless Lord-
And King of my heart may He ever be.

Oh, there is a yellow buttercup-
It brings to mind that golden street
Which I shall walk in Heaven above,
Where my blessed Savior I shall meet.

The white rose stands for purity,
To me it can never mean anything less
Than that I'm pure in the sight of God,
For I stand in Christ's own righteousness.

*Gary's note: She taught me to see the beauty of
God's creation and it stood me well as a
photographer in later life. I owe much to my
God and the mother he gave!*

God's Way
1947

"This is <u>the</u> way, walk ye in it." Isaiah 30:21

"Crushed 'neath the burdens you are called to
bear?"
<u>My</u> way is to cast upon me your care?
Disappointed because the path is so rough?
<u>My</u> way is perfect - is not that enough?
Tired in body, in mind distressed?
<u>My</u> way says, "come unto me and rest."
Afraid for the future, hopes in dust laid?
<u>My</u> word instructs thee to "be not afraid",
Under the pressure, fearful of failing me?
<u>My</u> promise, "my grace is sufficient for thee."
Perplexed, questioning the reason why?
That this is <u>my</u> way should satisfy.
Sick with the helplessness of regret?
<u>My</u> way is press onward, the past forget."

Whatever may come, "this is <u>the</u> way,
Walk ye in it," to me Thou dost say;
I stand rebuked, my precious Lord --
Peace and confidence are restored.

199

Going On

"Rise, let us be going." Matthew 26:46

They fell asleep, disciples tired and weary;
Demands of flesh had proved too much for
them;
Awakened by His word, and sore chagrined,
They almost wishes this time He would
condemn.
But Jesus spoke to them only to say,
"This time is lost, forever passed away;
Let not your sorrow turn into despair,
But rise up now, let us be on our way."

Once I, too, drifted deep in lethargy,
Onslaughts of sin unable to resist;
Forgiven and restored, yet still despairing,
I thought all chance for service I had missed.
There to me those selfsame words He gave,
"Rise, and go to do the duty at hand;
The past cannot be altered or recalled -
Let us go on to other tasks I've planned."

*Gary's Note: Her regret at the "call of
missions" lost.*

200

Good Cheer
"Be of good cheer." John 16:33

Sometimes I am downcast because I fail
Over some sin in my life to prevail   --
I long to attain more complete victory,
For my sinfulness often distresses me;
    But I have learned full well
    Through many a troubled year
    To trust my God in sorrow,
    Ever to be of good cheer.

I have small success winning souls for God,
But when I bow 'neath His chastening rod,
The peace the Lord gives I can make manifest,
Prove his grace is sufficient for each test;
    To others I can witness
    Of a Comforter divine,
    And tell how in the trouble
    His wonderful joy is mine.

The things I long here for my Savior to do
Are often never accomplished, it's true;
But in grief I can carry a cheerful face,
All submissive tears shed in the secret place;
    The wonder of His comfort
    That is found in every trial
    I can always show to others
    By just a cheery smile.

Heart Searching

What does the world think of me?
With that I am not concerned;
But what do they think of the God I serve?
What of Him have they learned
From observing the life that I live
Here day by day before men?
"Am I reflecting the glory of God?"
Is the real question then.

In His love so shed abroad in my heart
That it reaches out to say
To whomever may contact,
God loves in an infinite way?
Is my spirit one of forgiveness
Although I may have been wronged,
Revealing to others that mercy
Has ever to God belonged.

Yet can I chastise when needed
Those e'er whom I have control,
Showing that there is a reckoning
With God for every soul?
Thus speak to all around me
That sin bears a penalty,
That because Jesus paid the price,
Men only through Him are free.

Can men trust fully the word I speak,
Realize that the reason why

Is only Jesus who is the truth,
They on His Word can rely?
Much is contained in my question;
Holy Spirit, the power is of Thee—
Make me to reflect God's image
In my measure of capacity.

He Calleth for Thee

"The Master is come and calleth for thee." John 11:28

The Master is come, lost sinner;
He came to die in your place,
To take your sin upon Himself -
Matchless example of grace!
He calleth for thee to receive
And I ever unto Him to cleave.

The Master is come to your heart -
Christian, He calleth for thee
To live that He may be honored
Through life and eternity;
He wants you to surrender all -
Will you answer "yes" to His call?

The Master is come, troubled one,
To ease your heartache and pain,
To turn all your grief into joy,
As He sends sun after rain;
He calleth thee not to despair,
But to cast upon Him your care.

The Master is come and gives you
His salvation, joy, and peace;
He satisfies every longing,
And from guilt He brings release;
He calleth for thee to declare;
This blessed message everywhere.

Some blest day the cry, "He is come -
He calleth for thee above,
To live in a home in heaven,
Prepared by His hands of love,"
Will come to make your heart rejoice
That on earth you heeded His voice.

He Hears

"I have heard thy prayers, I have seen thy
tears." Is. 38:5

Have you earnestly prayed, and still the Lord
Seems never to hear your cry
For the salvation of loved ones dear?
Are you tempted to ask why?
Although your tears are flowing fast,
God sees and also hears,
For He says," I have heard thy prayers,
And I have seen thy tears."

Are you discouraged when life is hard?
Are tirals and tears your lot?
Have you cried to God for deliverance,
And yet He has answered not?
Learn quiet submission unto Him
When life's trouble appears,
For He says, "I have heard thy prayers,
And I have seen thy tears."

Have you longingly prayed for victory,
And yielded yourself to Him,
But often tears flow because of your sins?
Is hope of o'ercoming dim?
God is fulfilling His work in you;
The end of His plan nears,
For He says, "I have heard thy prayer,
And I have seen thy tears."

He Will Come

"I will come again." John 14:6

He will come-and all the weary days
Of toil, of heartache, or of pain
Will be forgotten in His presence,
For He said, "I will come again,"

He will come-and the pain of parting
From loved ones nevermore will be;
Parting then to break the heart,
But fellowship eternally.

He will come-and no more bitter tears
Will fall in grief from eyes grown dim,
And no more night of woe will ever be,
When he receives us unto Him.

He will come-there shall be no more death
To darken lives, no, nevermore!
But we shall reunite with those
Who have gone on to heaven before.

He will come-and all the useless wars
And misery of war shall cease,
And peace shall reign up on the earth,
When He shall come, the Prince of peace.

He will come-Lord Jesus, quickly come!
Come quickly, take us home with Thee!
No sorrow, nor sighing, no tears nor pain-
Lord, soon may Thy coming be!

His Presence

When I come into God's presence
And there's nothing in between,
Just to revel in His beauty,
To commune with the Unseen,
Awe and reverence fill my spirit,
As I worship and adore,
Enveloped in His love,
"More of Thee," my heart cries, "more!"

Though I have no plea to offer,
Though He may not speak a word,
Flooded with Himself alone,
There on me is grace conferred.
The blest glory of His presence
Holds a sweetness undefined
That permeates my being,
All my body, heart and mind.

The radiance of His person,
As I bow in silence, still,
Imparts a glorious rapture,
And subjected is my will;
All things pale before His presence
Like the mist before the sun;
Only He is all-important,
The all-sufficient One.

Gary's note: she was a worshipper of Almighty God. What a heritage we as her children enjoy!

I Change Not

"For I am the Lord, I change not." Mal. 3:6

"I change not; because I have allowed
The sun to be obscured by the cloud,
Has then the light gone from the sky?
No, it is there, and so am I.
When troubles come, as troubles will,
I never change, I am here still.

"I change not; when snow covers the land,
Will there never be ground on which to stand?
Yes, earth is as firm as it ever was,
And I change not, though the circumstance does.
In the world you shall have tribulation,
But I am with you in every situation.

"I change not; though each night it is dark,
This does not the end of everything mark-
The trees and grass and street are yet there,
And so am I near you to love and care,
To comfort, uphold, give strength and grace,
Though you sometimes walk through a darkened
place."

I Have Jesus

I have no riches, while others have wealth,
And I have sickness, while others have health,
    But I have Jesus.
Many see loved ones every day;
Mothers can guide each child on the way-
Leaving my children to another's care,
I am content with a glimpse here and there,
    For I have Jesus.

Others have sometime a sorrow to bear,
With no place of refuge, no one to share,
    But I have Jesus.
At times sore trials must come to all,
But some have no one on whom to call;
There are many bowed down beneath some care,
Knowing not the One to turn to in prayer,
    But I have Jesus.

Many still carry the load of their sin,
But I am saved, have new life within,
    For I have Jesus.
Many know not of the love of Christ,
That He for sin His life sacrificed,
Do not know that He came to die in their place,
Know not what it means to be "saved by grace,"
    But I have Jesus.

How thankful I am that He is so near!
How grateful I am He banishes fear,

That I have Jesus!
I have a Refuge from grief and cares;
I am God's child, He answers my prayers;
There's a song on my lips, joy in my heart;
I have a peace that will never depart,
      Because I have Jesus.

I long to see others share in this joy,
This peace that nothing on earth can destroy,
      To see them find Jesus,
To help them to find this comfort in Him,
If their ways lead them through shadows dim;
Lord, use me to teach transgressors Thy way,
To help them to claim this salvation today,
      Found only in Jesus.

Is It I?

"He said...one of you shall betray me...and began everyone of them to say unto Him, Lord, is it I?" Mt. 26:21, 22

"Lord, is it I?" Oh, how the question burns,
And with strong conviction to my soul returns!
"Lord, is it I?" It comes now with such force
That the very thought strikes to my heart remorse.
"Lord, is it I?" I, too, this query make,
"Betray I the One who died for my own sake?"

Lord, it is I! I bow my head in shame,
For I often bring dishonor to Thy name;
Often it is I who in my stubborn pride
Walk in my own way and fail to let Thee guide;
Often it is I who speak the angry word,
Or commit the act by which some strife is stirred.

Yes, Lord, it is I who fail to testify
Of Thy saving power, and Lord, it is I
Who know to do the good and shirk the duty still,
Who will not surrender wholly to Thy will,
I who take so little time to watch and pray
Or to do Thy work-thus do I betray.

But Lord it is I who, with a sorrowful tear,
Bow to ask forgiveness from a heart sincere,
Ask Thee now for cleansing and for victory-

For Thou knowest truly that I do love Thee;
As I now confess, I see Thy Book within:
"The blood of Jesus Christ cleanseth from all sin."

I Would See Jesus

"Sir, we would see Jesus." John 12:21

I would see Jesus when temptations rise:
The urge to speak sharp words or little lies;
Failure, through fear, to say the word I might;
Impulse to argue when I think I'm right;
Whenever I am tempted to do wrong,
I would see Jesus that I might be strong.

I would see Jesus when I've cause to fear;
I would be conscious He is standing near
Who said, "I will not fail thee, nor forsake,"
Who also said He knows the way I take;
I would trust Him what time I am afraid-
If I see Jesus, all my fears will fade.

I would see Jesus in the midst of care;
When problems arise, I would find Him in prayer;
When strength has failed me for the daily task
And I am tempted "why?" of God to ask;
When my heart faints, by heavy burdens pressed,
I would see Jesus, finding in Him rest.

I would see Jesus Christ in everything,
For only He can lessen sorrow's sting;
Jesus alone gives patience to endure
And power to resist temptation's lure;
One glimpse of Christ causes my heart to sing-
I would ever see Him as my Lord and King.

Jesus Speaks

"Present your bodies...unto God." Romans 12:1

"I walked this earth once long ago
In a body prepared for Me
To heal the broken-hearted
And set sin's captives free;
I preached the remedy for sin;
I came to do God's will;
But now that I've returned to heaven,
I need a body still.

"I still need someone here on earth
Who will let Me come in
In all the fullness of My power
To free that life from sin;
I need this one to contact men
And show them to My love;
I need a body to take My place,
Since I have gone above.

"I need cleansed lips to speak My words,
A heart through which to pray;
I need feet willing to walk like mine
In holiness each day;
I need a body I can live in –
Will Thou not lend Me thine?"
Yes! Lord, live out your life today
In this body of mine.

Learning

"-and learn of Me." Mt. 11:29

"Learn of Me concern for dying souls:
Hear again My mournful, saddened cry,
Lamenting o'er Jerusalem for those
Who spurned My love, preferring thus to die.
Learn of Me to love when others hate:
See Me dying for My enemies.
Look at Me, fatigued from doing good,
And nevermore can you live on in ease.

"Learn of Me to pray for darkened hearts:
I prayed whole nights when I needed rest,
And in Gethsemane I agonized,
Gaining triumph in that bitter test;
Learn of Me the secret of submission
To the will of God for every day.
My prayers were for My Father's glory;
Learn of Me-I will teach you to pray.

"Learn of Me to go to Calvary's cross,
Offer up yourself and die with Me,
Desires of the flesh there crucified-
Then rise to live henceforth triumphantly.
Yes, learn of Me all along your pathway:
I know all of your infirmity-
I came to live as man so that you could
From My life and service learn of Me."

Limiting God

"They...limited the Holy One of Israel." Ps. 78:41
(After reading a chapter in the book, "In His Presence," by Anna J. Lindgren.)

"With My own blessing and fullness
I would have filled you, child of Mine,
Have taken complete possession,
Brightly made your light to shine;
It was not a limited capacity
That hindered My working in you,
But you would not yield your littleness
As a channel I might work through.

"I wanted to make you a spring
That to others would overflow—
You chose to be a reservoir
Where water is stagnant and low;
Through you I meant to bless others—
For self a blessing you sought;
I wanted My power released through prayer—
You prayed because you ought.

"I would have made you My mouthpiece,
Speaking forth My word so free,
Convicting, saving, comforting—
Your lack of faith limited Me;
I would have made you a whirlwind
To shake, uproot, sweep clean—
You chose to be a nice little breeze
That would keep men calm and serene.

"But it is not too late, My child,
If you seek My best to obtain;
Much of your life has been wasted-
Give to Me the days that remain.
Will you turn from what men are saying,
Attune your ear to My voice,
Seek Me with undivided heart,
Dare to make My best your choice?

"Will you ignore men's opinions,
Cease to bow to the popular,
Not dabble in vain philosophies,
But the Spirit's power prefer?
Then trust Me for the impossible,
Child born of My infinite love;
And do not fear, stand still and see
My power now sent from above!"

Marvel

"I marvel that ye are so soon removed from Him." Gal. 1:6

So soon, so soon I am removed from Him
Unto the sinful thought, or word, or deed,
Deserting Christ and fellowship with Him,
To crucify afresh by the misdeed.

I marvel that so soon removed from Him,
Inclined to let things crowd Him out somehow,
So soon I give less heed to His commands,
Too soon I must confess the broken vow.

Then suddenly removed from Him again,
I do the thing contrary to His will,
Forsaking the Lord's way in willfulness,
Drawn to the world that holds attraction still.

Sometimes, all unaware, removed from Him,
Not to some other doctrine I have been,
But unto selfish living and obtaining,
Forgetting there are others yet to win.

Too often I am soon removed from Him
Unto enjoying pleasures that are right,
But leave less time to read the Word and pray…
Thus take the good, while of His best lose sight.

But some day I shall be removed from earth,
And from this sinful straying every day,
Unto the presence of the Lord in heaven,
Never again removed from Him away.

Misplaced Knowledge

We Christians know more of some books
Than we do of the Word of God;
We know more about some magazines-
The Lord must think that odd!
We know some of Christ and His gospel,
But more of the daily news,
Know more of some things than is good for us-
Too seldom the best we choose.

Women spend time in cooking meals
(for our families must be fed),
And yet neglect to feed their souls
On Christ Jesus, the living Bread;
We wash the clothes and mop up the floors,
Dust shelves that are seldom seen,
But find little time to open our hearts
To the Word which washes clean.

Men learn to conduct their business,
With earthly success as their goal,
But have no time for the greater need,
The business of winning a soul;
They study how to win more friends
And influence people of earth,
Yet care less for the approval of God,
A thing of far greater worth.

Christians have learned about many things-
We are proud of our knowledge, too;

But we need to learn more of some things
That would prove of greater value:
Much more of a closer walk with God,
More of how to watch and pray,
More of how to win a soul to Christ,
More of victory each day.

Modern Thought

"Thus saith the Lord, 'Stand ye in the ways, and see, and ask for the old paths, where is the good way, and walk therein, and ye shall find rest for your souls.' But they said, 'We will not walk therein.'" Jer. 6:16

They say to God, "We will not walk therein;
We will not tread the paths of truth and light,
For we have found new ways that suit our taste,
And look with pity from our learned height
On those who dare to choose the old and true,
To stand on what is written in God's Word;
For we are wise (they say!) and thus we teach
To follow in the old ways is absurd."

But the Lord warns, "If you walk not therein,
But choose instead the path of vanity,
You will continue to be desolate.
Seeking peace of heart continually,
But cannot find, because you seek it not
In Me and in the way I have set;
Never shall there be rest for your souls,
Your lives will be filled up with care and fret."

My God

My Savior is a God of love
Love giving and commanding; (2 Corinthians
13:11)
He is to me the God of Peace,
Peace past all understanding; (Hebrews 13:20
He is a God of patience, too,
Longsuffering toward all, (Romans 15:5)
Willing to be the God of hope
To any who will call; (Romans 15:13)
I pray before the God of heaven,
Who hears my every plea, (Neh. 1:4)
For this God of hosts majestic
A Father is to me, (Psalms 80:7)
God of all grace, sufficient
In every situation, (1 Peter 5:10)
God of all comfort in distress,
Yea, God of consolation. (2 Corinthians 1: 3,
Romans 15:5)

My Prayer

Lord, take my life and make it
What Thou wouldst have it be;
Take it, and may it always
Be a true witness for thee.

Help me ever to be true,
Loving, unselfish, and kind,
That those who know thee not
Thy likeness in me may find.

Help me to speak the words
That thou wouldst have me say,
To do things for the advancement
Of thy cause, day by day.

And above all, I pray, dear Lord,
To win others I may endeavor,
To bring lost souls to Christ-
And thine be the praise forever.

Need

"My God shall supply all your need." Phil. 4:19

I needed strength
To bear the sorrow pressing on my aching heart,
And when I went to be quietly with Him apart,
He gave not only strength my burden to bear,
But quietness, and peace, and joy beyond
compare.

I needed cleansing,
For I had sinned and sorely grieved my Lord, I
knew,
And my heart was very heavy with the
knowledge, too;
So I sought His face, and there my sin
confessed,
Then fellowship with Him restored, my heart
found rest.

I needed grace
To overcome bitterness, springing up within
Because of some wrong...for I knew it was sin;
When I heard His voice to me, speaking through
the Book,
"Love your enemies," I found grace to overlook.

I needed love,
Love that endures all things, suffers long, is
kind,
Love that never fails and no evil seeks to find,

A deeper love for the Lord and for my fellow
man...
This love He often gave me o'er and o'er again.

    I needed patience
For my daily walk, because the tasks were
trying,
And for guidance those I love were on me
relying,
But He only sent more trials and from these I
learned
Tribulation works that patience for which I
yearned.

    Whatever is my need,
For body or for soul, He everything supplies,
Not always what I want-for that He is too wise-
But just the thing He knows will be the best for
me;
Exceeding all I ask or think, He gives
abundantly.

Night

I thank God for the quietness of night;
After the noise and turmoil of the day,
Darkness is rest for tired eyes and nerves,
And in the silence there is time to pray.

How wonderful the blessed quietness!
The little worries and anxieties
Vanish away, committed unto God,
Rest and peace taking the place of these.

The penetrating stillness all about
Gently enters my soul to stay,
To be the quietness and confidence
That shall make up my strength another day.

Gary's Note: Written while she was single and living alone, while working at the dorms at Oregon State University in the 1960/70's?

One More Day

I will have faith in God for one more day,
Though weary, painful, rugged is my way;
As now across my path the shadows fall,
Once more He will give strength to face it all,
That I may prove to those who know Christ not
That He is real, not just figment of thought.

And I will show to others round about
That it is foolishness ever to doubt,
For God can fill the need of every heart,
Can to the trusting one His peace impart;
Though easier to cry once in awhile,
For one more day I will display a smile.

For one more day God has power to give
Grace for me victoriously to live;
For one more day I know He will be near
To uphold me, to comfort, and to cheer;
So I will do my best in every way
To glorify my Lord for one more day.

Patience

So often I prayed for patience,
And yet I failed to see
That I had made much progress
Toward what I long to be.

For only trouble and heartache
And trials come my way,
Till I had need of patience
To bear them day by day.

"Tribulation worketh patience,"
Thus does God's Word declare,
So perhaps this tribulation
Is answer to my prayer!

Perspective

A glistening page-
With one ink spot-
Yet all we see
As often as not
Is that dark blot.

Abundant blessings-
Do we lament,
Focus upon
One element
Of discontent?

Restoration

"And they all forsook Him and fled."
Mark 14:50

They walked and talked in Galilee
With Christ the Son of man;
They knew the sweetness of fellowship
Only disciples can;
They saw His miracles in lives
That they had brought to Him,
His Word light up the lamp of faith
In hearts where it was dim.

They watched while souls sick of there sin
Arose out of defeat,
And helped Him feed the hungry ones
Till satisfied complete.
They saw Him drive the devils out,
When they were powerless;
They prayed with Him (He taught them how),
They failed through prayerlessness!

And yet-and yet-how sad the words.
That "All forsook Him and fled,"
Even Peter and John, who loved Him most-
How His heart must have bled!
But-is there one of all God's saints
Who sometimes has not failed,
Whose love for Him stood not the test,
And sin in heart prevailed?

Hope shines for the sufferer,
The soul sick with regret:
Christ's special words to Peter,
"Fear not; for I live yet."
He dwells with the contrite one (Isaiah 57:15)
Whose heart with sorrow breaks,
To give some greater work to do,
To overrule mistakes.

Romans 12

I plead with you by the mercies of God
That your bodies you wholly present
As a living sacrifice to Him
To this reasonable service consent.
To prove the perfect will of God
To this world be not conformed
But by the renewing of your mind
Through His Spirit be transformed
I, Paul say to every man
Through the grace given to me
Not to think of himself too highly
But consider soberly
As each body has many members
But their work is not the same
We are members of one another
The Body of Christ to frame-
And having different gifts,
If through grace given prophecy
Let us prophesy in faith,
Minister with proficiency.
The one who is called as a teacher
Must his learning communicate
If another is chosen to exhort
An exhortation let him wait
He that rules, let Him do it
With all diligence; and he
Showing mercy, do it with cheerfulness
He that giveth, with simplicity
Let there be in love no hypocrisy

Cleave to the good, all evil abhor
Be kindly affectioned to each other
Willing that others be to the fore
Be not slothful in business
But fervent in spirit, rejoicing in hope
Serving the Lord and instant in prayer
Patient in all tribulations scope
Be not wanting in hospitality.

Salvation

"Believe on the Lord Jesus Christ, and thou
shalt be saved." Acts 16:31

"Believe"-just trust in Christ
Who died to save your soul;
Believe, because God sayest 'tis so,
That He will make you whole;
When you believing come,
Your faith He will reward,
So do not wait for feeling-
Just leave that to the Lord.

"Believe on the Lord Jesus Christ;"
The workings of His grace
You need not understand;
Believe He took your place,
And became your substitute;
Because He died for you,
God forgives if you believe-
'Tis all you need to do.

"And thou-" you who have so long
Refused to take Him in,
Have rejected Him thru all the years,
Preferred to stay in sin
You does he love so, that He
Came from Heaven on high
To redeem you from all sin,
Came in your place to die.

Thus "thou shalt be saved"- saved from
The penalty of sin;
"The wages of sin is death,"
But eternal life you win
If you accept the Savior-
The pardon you desire
Is yours-"thou shalt be saved"
From death and from hell fire.

Silver Surf

I love the pounding silver surf
Dancing with joy in sunlight
I see persistence thus portrayed
In each singing wave of white;
These sea ranges of lovliness,
White with capes of foamy snow,
Tell much of the power of God
To thoughtful watchers.

Moving breakers raising a song
Pushing on to white gold sand
Scurrying to catch each other
Speak words I understand;
Like little curtsying angels
Poised on platinum wings
All their crests of foaming silver
Remind of heavenly things.

Endless ribbons of silver hue
Replicas of each other
Seeking ever the silent shore
Waving to one another-
These waves of ceaseless energy
No resting place can find.
Like rushing about to still
Longings of heart and mind

Lift their sparking heads to view
Then they plunge in abandon

Into waiting arms of blue
Just as the sinner cast himself
Into the sea of God's love,
Finds assurance of forgiveness
And joy he never dreamed of.

Submission

Gladly I said the words, "Not my will, but
Thine, be done."
To God this promise made, as the new year was
begun;
It seemed very easy then, when all was going
right,
To yield everything to Him and in His will
delight.

Firmly I iterated once more to Him the vow,
When I found that I must spend more time in
praying now,
And do many things that I had before neglected,
But doing His will brought more joy than I
expected.

"Not my will, but Thine, be done," I said
reluctantly,
When many little trials crowded in upon me;
Yet I knew these things were working only for
my good,
So relying on this knowledge, resolute I stood.

Sadly I said again, with my heart nearly
breaking,
"Not my will, but Thine, be done," new
surrender making;
I felt the Lord was putting my faith unto the
test,

Therefore I found comfort in trusting His way is best.

"Not my will, but Thine, be done," I cried in near despair,
As I faced the vale of death, with darkness everywhere;
Then He calmed all my fears and gave a glimpse to me,
Of what it will mean in heaven with Jesus to be.

"Not my will, but Thine, be done," has daily been the key,
By which I have received all the blessings given me;
I have a greater peace and my heart is full of praise;
Awe and wonder fill me at the working of His ways.

The Appointed Place

We are not set in our appointed place
Just to enjoy a selfish life of ease;
Jesus has called us out of death to life
To do His will, and not ourselves to please.
Who has a better right therefore to choose
What that place of service for Him be?
Because He surely knows where He needs you,
And He knows best where He has need of me.

He gives to one the ministry of prayer
Who's laid aside upon a bed of pain;
Another has a place of prominence;
Some ever in the background must remain;
And yet another never gets beyond
Serving needs of home and family;
But always He knows best where to use you,
He knows how to make best use of me.

There may be one who cannot testify
Save by the life he displays before men;
While someone else may have a ready tongue;
And still another one a gifted pen;
He may call me to stay at home to serve;
He may send you far off across the sea;
But whether here or there we work for Him,
He knows the special place for you or me.

I think when we are tempted to rebel
At some untoward and trying circumstance,

We'd do well to carefully consider
That these things never come to us by chance;
It's wonderful to know the Lord can find
Spheres of service just for such as we,
That He knows best where He has need of you,
He knows well where He has need of me.

The Cost

I made this prayer to God, "Whatever the cost
may be,
Whatever the cost I want a closer walk with
Thee.
I am not satisfied today; I want new heights to
scale,
To live a more victorious life, where now I often
fail;
I want a truer witness to be, and I earnestly
pray,
Whatever the cost, O Lord, teach me the
overcoming way."

"Whatever the cost!" How high the price I knew
not then,
But what I have asked of God I will not take
back again.
What though He's taken me at my word and
answered my plea
With added trial and sorrow, shall I rebellious
be?
No! If through affliction and heartache the life I
desire be won,
If this be the road to victory...then, Lord, Thy
will be done!

The Healer

"He hath sent Me to heal the broken-hearted."
Luke 4:18

There are so many things to break the heart
In naming them there seems no place to start:
Harsh words unjustly spoken cut for years;
Hard words that show no love can bring the
tears;
Words can wield such careless, brutal blows
To crush a heart that never hardened grows.

And there is such variety of things
To cause dismay life almost daily brings;
Problems arise and there is none to aid;
And every day another hope must face;
Life holds much grief when there is none to
care,
No earthly one who can our burdens share.

Hearts are filled with lots of broken things:
Memory of broken vows that stings;
Broken dreams where fault is all our own;
Crumbled hopes that wring from one a moan;
Failing faith of men is there often, too;
Or broken fellowship with God to rue.

Just One there is who will each sorrow share:
Christ can heal the wounds, the cracks repair;
Only He can mend the shattered parts,
Apply a soothing balm to pain-torn hearts;
Every grief of ours-and more-He knew,
For, you know, His heart was broken, too.

The Samaritan
Luke 10:30-37

The world is full of people hurt
In countless ways, though tragic blows,
Hurts of body and heart and mind—
All of these wounds the world knows;
What does it mean to you and to me?

The world is full of heartless ones,
Who care not for the other's pain,
Selfish, grasping, only intent
On pleasure, appetite, or gain;
God forbid that this should be
A picture of you, or of me.

The world is full of heedless men,
Who close their hearts and shut their eyes
To the sorrow all around them
Whose ears are deaf unto cries;
Shame should come to you and me,
If we're heedless of any misery.

The world has some helping hands,
Who carry the cross to those in need;
These carry to men a loving Christ
Who alone can comfort hearts that bleed;
Do those hands belong to you and me?
Or do we ignore their silent plea?

The Same Jesus
"Jesus Christ is the same yesterday, today, and forever."
Hebrews 13:8

Yesterday He eased my heartache;
Yesterday He stilled my fears;
Yesterday He whispered to me
That every prayer He hears;
Yesterday He travelled with me,
And His presence comfort brought,
Gave assurance that He loves me,
Though my ways with trial fraught.

Yesterday when I was wretched,
Lovingly He dried my tears,
And I knew, because He reigns,
Life's not bleak as it appears;
Yesterday He took my problems
On Himself and bade me cease
From endeavoring to solve them,
Bade me know He keeps the keys.

Yesterday in all the darkness
His glorious light shined through;
And yesterday He gave me strength
For my weakest moment, too;
Yesterday to all my lonliness
He so graciously gave heed...
He came to fill my lonely heart
And prove He is all I need.

Yesterday a loving Father
All my varied needs supplied,
So today again I'll trust Him,
Thus in perfect peace abide;
If the Lord was all-sufficient
For the needs of yesterday,
Surely I can safely trust Him
To be just the same today.

The Strength of the Lord

"I will go in the strength of the Lord God."
Psalms 71:16

I will go in the strength of the Lord
Through routine tasks of the day,
Every little thing I must do
Done in my very best way;
For there can never be monotony
While my Lord, Christ Jesus, dwells with me.

I will go in the strength of the Lord
Through lonliness or through loss;
He knows how hot the fire must be
To purge away any dross;
His love and mercy ever sustain....
What seems loss will mean greater gain.

I will go in the strength of the Lord
Go on yet praying I will,
Though the one prayer nearest my heart
Seems to be unheeded still;
Because I have proved His Word before,
I know He'll give all I ask, and more.

I will go in the strength of the Lord
To tell of His love and grace,
To live that He may be honored,
Then soon I shall see His face;
Whatever conditions life may afford,
I will ever go in the strength of the Lord.

The Twenty-third Psalm

The Lord is my Shepherd:
I shall not know need;
I rest in green pastures,
And me He doth lead
By still, peaceful waters;
And for His name's sake
He leadeth me on
In righteousness' wake;
If I stray, He restores me.
No evil I'll fear,
Tho' I walk thru death's valley;
He ever is near
To support and uphold
With His staff and His rod,
To encourage my soul
With the comfort of God.
I feed from a table
Prepared by His love;
He anointest my head
With oil from above;
My cup runneth over
With joy and with peace.
His goodness and mercy
He never will cease
All the days of my life;
And when breaketh life's cord,
Forever I'll dwell
In the house of the Lord.

The Two Stars

The eastern kings had waited long-
When they beheld the star,
Their purpose was to worship Christ,
Though they must travel far.
The Star out of Jacob has come,
The Bright and morning Star;
Will you leave all to worship Him,
Coming just as you are?

The wise men had brought from the East
Gifts for the little Boy,
So when they saw His star appear,
They rejoiced with great joy;
If you bring the gift of yourself,
The Day Star will arise
In your heart to give you the joy
And peace that satisfies.

On their journey both night and day,
The star went before them,
Till the Child they had been seeking
They found at Bethlehem;
All the way from earth to heaven
Christ has gone on before-
He calls you now to follow Him,
This Bethlehem's Savior.

The Unanswered Call

The Lord called me to go to far off China;
Years ago I heard Him speak to me,
But there were other claims upon my life-
Perhaps it was God's plan that this should be,
Or-just perhaps-I put others before Him,
But the fact remains I did not go
To tell the story of His love and grace,
That China might the name of Jesus know.

Now that land is torn by bitter suffering-
Communists have come to take control;
Not having God, they followed a delusion,
And a dagger of remorse pierces my soul.
Maybe there were scores of others like me
Who never heeded when they heard God call-
Had we gone then to tell salvation's story,
To Godless hands would China's millions fall?

If you are looking toward the mission field,
Let nothing, nothing else come in between,
For only He knows where you are most needed;
Consider well therefore what it might mean
To fail to go to those who sit in darkness;
Never be deflected from your course,
Lest you in later years regret your folly,
Your heart be filled up with futile remorse.

*Author's note: Written soon after the
Communists took over control of China*

The Weather

It seems we're never satisfied
In any kind of weather;
It doesn't seem to matter much
If it is cold, or whether
The sun is shining brightly,
Or the rain comes pouring down,
We just are never satisfied,
We grumble or we frown.

If it's foggy or it's cloudy,
Then we wish the sun would shine,
But if the sun obliges us,
Then do we think it's fine?
Oh, no! We keep on grumbling—
Now we simply must complain
That it's too hot or it's too dry,
And we wish that it would rain.

We find it just the same in life,
Whether it is dark or fair;
We fancy we could do without
The burdens that we bear,
Yet find life too monotonous
When it is as fair as May,
For we would like to manage
Our lives in our selfish way.

But God, who makes the universe
In every kind of weather,

Who knows what's best in natures realm,
Makes all things work together
For good to those who love
The Lord devotedly;
He who controls the weather
Will care well for you and me.

Thoughts on Easter Day

Lovely, warming sunshine, streaming from on
high,
Brings to mind the love and light Jesus does
supply:
Love, because He came to earth to take the
sinners' place,
Die for us that we might know that love, shown
by His grace;
Light, because He is the One who takes away
the gloom
Of death, for He arose victorious from the tomb.

Gentle cooling breezes, blowing on my cheek,
Of the Holy Spirit seem to me to speak,
For He comes in gently, when faith unlocks the
door,
To dwell within our hearts, a Holy Conqueror;
Yet this same Holy Spirit raised Jesus from the
dead
To free us evermore from all our fear and
dread.

Yellow, blooming jonquils, nodding in the breeze,
And the fragrant violets drive me to my knees
To thank my Father God for the beauty of the
spring,
For the glorious promise in earth's awakening,
The promise of eternal life Christ's resurrection
gives:
That we have hope of heaven because we know
He lives.

To Ruth

(A friend who has been <u>seven years</u> in a T.B. Hospital)

Of times when I'm tempted my lot to bewail,
One remedy truly seems never to fail:
I think of <u>you</u> valiantly fighting for health,
Yet bravely disdaining to pity yourself;
Using your trial from day to day
As a stepping stone on your heavenward way;
Smiling, though lonely, and laughing, though weary,
Determined to stay courageous and cheery;
Asking no sympathy, waiting no praise,
Admiration compelling in countless ways;
Seeking this only God's Word to obey,
Walking with Him thru each passing day;
Patiently, sweetly resigned to His will,
Waiting until His design He fulfills;
Loyal and trustworthy, faithful and true-
These are some lessons I have learned from <u>you.</u>

Gary's Note: To Ruth (Horn)
Lesson learned: my mother's
recollections/impressions of this Godly woman's
testimony through trial. Would my mother
suffer the same fate?

Tragedy at Christmas

The Son of God looks down from heaven
Upon the earth to see
If any honor Him amid
Christmas festivity;
He looks on decorated homes,
On parties gay and mirth-
How many are remembering
To celebrate His birth?

Every family has a tree
All glittering and bright,
But seldom a Bible opened,
No manger scene in sight,
No worshipping a Savior, born
'Neath a star of Bethlehem,
Not "Silent Night," but "Jingle Bells,"
Means Christmas time to them.

He sees some signing Christmas cards
For friends both far and near,
And in Christ's searching eye just now
I think I see a tear;
There's Santa or a wintry scene
Depicted on the front,
But for a word of Scripture
Vainly does He hunt.

He watches presents being wrapped,
No thought of the One that's missed,

For He whose birthday is this day
Is not found on the list;
There are so few who recollect
Why Christmas gifts are given,
Even remember that first Gift
Which God sent down from heaven.

Jesus views the Christmas season
With sorrow in His heart,
For the real peace of Christmas
He only can impart;
One gift among the many here
Would fill heaven with gladness:
Your heart and life to Jesus give
To take away His sadness.

Traveling Abroad

I cannot be hemmed in by walls,
Because the whole wide world calls;
On wings of prayer I travel far
To where the missionaries are;
From land to land I fly about
To help in getting the gospel out;
Life cannot be uninteresting-
I am an ambassador for my King.

To devil-worshipping Africans,
Superstitious South Americans,
To India's hungry, sorrowing masses,
To crowded Formosan Bible classes
Anytime I choose I may quickly go,
Taking the remedy for their woe,
In prayer making known my one desire,
That God give workers souls for their hire.

Each day I visit such distant scenes
As the islands of the Philippines;
Often I journey to Japan,
Or the mountains of far Pakistan;
On Korean shores I dwell for long,
Then on to Burma or Hong Kong,
Perhaps to Jerusalem, or Rome-
Or pray just for the needs at home.

To China, whose need of God is certain,
To countries behind the iron curtain

I can carry the gospel's saving power
Just by praying one short hour;
When I uphold God's servants in prayer,
I somehow feel I have been there
To those strange lands across the foam —
I'm a world-traveler, though I stay at home!

Gary's note: The missionaries heart...I too have been allowed the ministry of prayer and recently learned, although persecuted, there are as many as 150 million Christian in China. Wonderful God!

Unscriptural

Untold millions in foreign lands
Are yet untold of nail-pierced hands,
Untaught of the only sacrifice,
That will for all their sins suffice,
Untold of the Savior of Calvary,
Who was bruised for their iniquity.

Uncounted numbers across the sea,
Masses of unloved humanity,
Who live in unbelievable sin,
Too long unapproached by us have been;
Unreached with the Gospel's saving power,
Unconverted hundreds die every hour.

Unending streams of men undone
(the task of saving them just begun)
An undreamed number in darkness reels;
Our praying undone, unconcern reveals.
Still undone the going, unpaid the cost
Yet unmeasured the worth of souls that are
lost.

Valleys

"Yea, though I walk through the valley-Thou
art with me." Ps. 32:4
"Every valley shall be exalted..." Is. 40:4

I have been in the valley of sin,
But Christ Jesus has lifted me,
Exalted to fellowship with Him,
God's heir with Him to be.

I have been through the vale of sorrow;
The God of comfort in sadness
There healed my broken heart,
Turning my mourning to gladness.

I have been in the valley of pain,
And like Paul I prayed it dpart;
Though often His answer was "no,"
He taught things dear to my heart.

I have been to the vale of weakness,
And found true His promise to me:
"My strength is made perfect in weakness,
My grace is sufficient for thee."

I have been through the valley of doubt,
Question there the way that I trod;
Soon I saw Him more clearly and cried,
Like Thomas, "My Lord and my God!"

I have been near the valley of death
And found I had nothing to fear,
For what is death to His child
But lifted to heaven from here?

All the valleys of trouble in life,
Though fearful, or painful, or dim
Are exalted places indeed,
For I am accompanied by Him.

What Do Ye More Than Others?
Matthew 5:47

What do you more than others
For the glory of the Lord?
Do you go the second mile,
His approval your reward?
A Christian should be different
From others round about–
Do your neighbors have a chance
To think of you with doubt?

If someone is unreasonable,
Do you give in with grace,
Or to hold your own determine,
For fear of losing face?
God must often times be grieved–
He expects of Christians more
Than a mere formal religion;
Are you different than before?

When you are persecuted
Just for doing what is right,
Is your heart filled up with anger?
How looks that in God's sight?
For a Christian is forgiving,
Must be gentle under stress,
Do good to those who hurt him,
Love his enemies, and bless.

What do you more than others?

Do you always keep your word?
Do you see to please yourself,
Or choose to please the Lord?
Do you e'er resist the evil
Done by others unto thee?
What do ye more than others?
Searching word for you and me!

What Sayest Thou?
"Wilt thou be made whole?" John 5:6

Wilt thou be made whole?
Sick unto death art thou,
Sick with sin and unbelief;
Death is thy portion now,
Except thou turn to Jesus
To heal your sin-sick soul.
What sayest thou, lost sinner?
Wilt thou be made whole?

The Great Physician waits
Only for you to call
Upon His holy name;
He tasted death for all-
All your souls diseases
And sins upon Him roll.
What sayest thou, lost sinner?
Wilt thou be made whole?

Sin has made deep wounds
Upon your heart and mind-
'Tis spiritual insanity'-
But he these wounds can bind;
The blood of Jesus can
Cleanse your guilty soul.
What sayest thou, lost sinner?
Wilt thou be made whole?

Whatever Jesus Does Is Right
"He hath done all things well," Mark 7:37

I know whatever Jesus does is right;
I will trust Him when troubled by fears;
When wave on waves comes the sea of trials,
And my eyes are washed by sudden tears,
When my heart grows weary and longs for the
time
That walking by faith changes to sight,
Still there is consciousness of His love,
For whatever Jesus does is right.

I know that whatever Jesus does is right;
I cannot question His plans for me;
Concern for my good He proved beyond doubt
By giving His life on Calvary.
Though the clouds of sorrow hover nearby,
Gather till my way grows dark as night,
There is peace in one quick, comforting thought,
That whatever Jesus does is right.

I know whatever Jesus does is right;
His wisdom knows no limitation;
His love is measured by His grace;
I find His Word true consolation,
A lamp to direct my stumbling feet,
A light e'er making the darkness bright;
Throughout life I have the sweet assurance
That whatever Jesus does is right.

Where is Thy Brother?
"Where is...thy brother?"   Gen. 4:9

Where is thy brother? Is he out in sin?
Have you made no effort to bring him in,
In through the Door of the sheepfold where
He, too, may know of the Shepherd's care?

Where is thy brother? Seeking the true way
To become reconciled to God? Oh, say,
Have you shown him the Word to help along,
Or let him go on in ways that are wrong?

Where is thy brother? Is sorrow his lot?
Have you shown the God of comfort? Why not?
You who have known God's comfort, can you
Keep silence when others need it, too?

Where is thy brother? Wandering away
From faith he once knew and straying today?
Do you condemn and do you deplore?
Or have you tried this one to restore?

Where is thy brother? The voice of God hear...
Your responsibility is made clear:
You know the Way to eternal life....
Tell it to those still in sin or strife.

Without Him

Comes a question to try imagination,
Bringing a sense of near desolation:
Without the Lord Jesus, what would I do?
He is Author of all joys that are true.
Without Him the day has no purpose, no aim,
No safety except His protection I claim,
No sense of His nearness in time of distress,
For my sins no atonement, no forgiveness.

Because I can say, "Thank you, Lord, for this,"
I find more pleasure in my child's kiss,
In an evening ride, my husband's love,
In music that lifts my thoughts above,
In my flower garden, a boy's joke,
The encouraging word that someone spoke.
How much more meaning to simple things
Pausing to thank the Savior brings.

What would it be like if I could not go
To God to tell Him all of my woe,
Receiving the comfort He only can give?
How, without prayer, could I ever live?
Yet around me are many who do not know
The joy of walking with my Lord so;
They are without Him-may I help them to see
This Savior who means so much to me.

Spring

"I thought of the verse in Gen. 8: 22, 'While the earth remaineth...summer and winter...shall not cease.' I wrote down my thoughts in a bit of a rhyming verse." -FFW

It <u>will</u> be spring again,
The bare bough leaf once more,
The singing of the birds be heard
Where it was stilled before;
There'll come a day when barren roots
Will spring to life at last,
When blossoms brighten up the earth,
And winter will be past.

It <u>will</u> be spring again;
Though winter snows now fall,
Sometime they'll melt beneath spring's sun;
Though storm and wind appall,
One day the gentle breeze of spring
Will blow dark clouds away,
Its warmth delight the heart of us
Much more for the delay.

It <u>will</u> be spring again;
Though barren now my soul,
New shoots of faith will spring anew,
God's promises console;
It will be spring again, the singing heart return;
Though for a season I must grieve,
A new song I will learn.

It <u>will</u> be spring again;
When dreariness of life
Sometimes chills to such despair,
Or cuts as with a knife,
God's love will warm my hopelessness,
To life new meaning bring.
How do I know? Winter does pass,
Then always comes the spring.

EDITOR'S NOTE

My father divorced my mother after thirty-one years of marriage. Devastated by the divorce and my father's rejection, Satan sowed seeds of dismay and sshe attempted suicide. She just wanted to go be with her Lord.

My mother and I were both helping in Bible school at our church, and when she did not show up I rushed home to find her foaming at the mouth and an empty bottle of sleeping pills on the night stand. However, God would not let her go that way.

Over time, God healed her of the heartache and she went into the workforce, though she had no formal training. God continued to lead her as she got a job as a desk clerk in a women's dormitory at Oregon State University. Later she became a house mother for Varsity House, a Christian home for young men attending OSU.

She thought she had failed her God, but God has a way of redeeming the lost years.

EPILOGUE

Florence Fern Austin-Wallace passed into the presence of her Lord and Savior, Jesus Christ, on April 11, 1988. In addition to the tuberculosis from which she had sufficiently recovered over the years, she had heart disease and around the time of her death could hardly walk across the room.

Her doctors were suggesting a new procedure called angioplasty (a balloon is inserted into a main artery and passed up to the blockage in the heart muscle, then inflated to open up the vessel to allow blood to flow again.) My mother had read up on the procedure and knew the risks for women were much higher than men.

She decided that she would only agree to the procedure if the doctors would agree to not resuscitate her if her heart stopped during the procedure. However, the doctors refused that stipulation. My mother reluctantly agreed to go ahead with the angioplasty, as it was very much needed. She wasn't afraid to die, as "to be absent from the body is to be present with the Lord."

During the procedure, her heart did indeed stop as she feared, though she was resuscitated. This caused additional suffering as the doctors attempted to remove fluid build-up in her damaged lungs. It did allow her youngest son, a pastor on the East Coast, to see her before she passed.

On that day I left the hospital for a few minutes. As I was returning, a perfect rainbow arched over the hospital. Tears filled my eyes as I then knew she would be in His presence soon.

As with many women and men of faith in the Lord Jesus Christ, their faith can be clearly seen, often for generations to come.

I am proud to have had Florence Fern Austin-Wallace as my mother. Really, though, she belonged to her Lord and I just got glimpses into her life.